never leave the

dogs behind

ALSO BY BRIANNA MADIA

Nowhere for Very Long

never leave the

dogs behind

A MEMOIR

brianna madia

HarperOne

An Imprint of HarperCollins*Publishers*

Excerpts of the 2018 essay "The Half-Wolves" by Emily Ruskovich included in Chapter 10 are printed with the permission of the author and NW Book Lovers.

HarperCollins books may be purchased for educational, business, or sales promotional use. For information, please email the Special Markets Department at SPsales@harpercollins.com.

FIRST HARPERCOLLINS PAPERBACK EDITION PUBLISHED IN 2025

Library of Congress Cataloging-in-Publication Data has been applied for.

ISBN 978-0-06-331610-2

25 26 27 28 29 LBC 5 4 3 2 1

FOR BUCKET, DAGWOOD,
BIRDIE, AND BANJO

Okay, thanks, guys

AUTHOR'S NOTE

This story contains mentions of depression and suicide. While I have done my best with the accuracy of details and timelines, please know that memories can often form imperfectly when we are simply trying to survive.

Most two-legged characters in this book have had their names changed to protect their identity.

It is a joy to be hidden,
and a disaster not to be found.

D. W. WINNICOTT

CONTENTS

Perhaps, in another life, you were a bird.
I can't be certain, but whoever you were, you must have been
terribly free.
A leash and four walls never suited you. Dog parks and paved
sidewalks were chaos for you to try and wrap your primitive,
untamed mind around.
In fact, sometimes I think I should have slid the collar from
your neck and turned you loose in the vast, silent openness of the
desert you love so deeply.
But I would have missed you too much.
So, I slipped my own collar and went with you instead.

chapter one

The Rounds

Every morning, my dog Dagwood made what I came to call "the rounds." As soon as the trailer door opened, he'd hop off the wooden deck, hook a left, then another left, before heading south toward the Abajo Mountains, their blue morning hue resting perfectly atop an otherwise flat horizon. I would watch his signature limp, the plate on his hind leg still visible at the top of his femur like half a golf ball beneath the skin. It never did quite go away after the accident.

The other three—Bucket, Birdie, and Banjo—usually kept a bit closer to the trailer. Birdie would skirt off behind her favorite boulder, her sanctuary for the privacy of a morning poop. Banjo, still only a few months old at the time, would toddle across the sand, nose to the ground, tracking one of the big black beetles he hadn't yet worked up the courage to try to eat. Bucket, ten years old and gray-faced, would position herself perfectly in the first patch of sun, paws crossed, eyes closed in bliss. But not Dagwood. Dagwood would turn to look at me just once before disappearing between the two-hundred-year-old juniper trees and patches of Mormon tea.

I was never quite sure where he went, but he'd always reappear a short while later, slack-jawed and satisfied that the perimeter of our nine-acre lot was clear. His ears always came into view first; the rising sun lit up the tips of them, as if he were glowing. *How'd it go, buddy?* I would ask. *Everything as it should be?*

The neighbors began voicing their frustrations with his morning wanderings when their motion-sensor wildlife cameras started catching his coyote-like body slinking past their porches. One night in the middle of August, a rainstorm turned to hail the size of dimes, bouncing off the metal roof of the trailer with such deafening fury that Dagwood burst through the screen door and took off into the dark. I ran after him screaming, soaking, covering my head from the pelting ice, but he ran faster than me, even with his bad leg. It was just past 11:00 p.m. when he tripped the porch light of a neighbor half a mile up the road. They called, shouting furiously into my voicemail about my dog waking them up. But I was busy driving up and down the flooding dirt road, calling his name from the window, trying to catch a glimpse of him in the purple flashes of lightning. A short while later, when I found him, I wanted to call back and explain that he was just scared. But any person who doesn't open a door for a dog in a hailstorm is not the kind of person who would care.

. . .

It didn't help that I'd never bothered to *meet* any of the neighbors, of course. Firstly, because their houses were far enough from my trailer that I couldn't see them in any direction, but mostly because I didn't move up there to have neighbors. And most of the time, I didn't. There were twenty lots on the mesa, each anywhere from eight to twenty-two acres. Some hadn't been developed at all, while others had ornate adobe homes or wooden cabins that looked like they would be better suited in Jackson Hole. Most of them sat empty for ten months a year. Vacation homes for folks whose *real* addresses were listed in California or Park City or New York. But in between the vacant mansions, there *were* a few folks up there on the mesa year-round. And—for increasingly obvious reasons—they didn't like me. And that was okay. I didn't like them either. By the time I wound up out there, I didn't like anybody.

In October (the mildest weather window in the desert) some of the lot owners came into town for the annual seventy-two hours they'd spend in their desert homes. Dagwood had been roving about for months by then and I'd never heard a word about it, so I continued to sit on the deck each morning with my coffee and one of my pet pythons around my neck while Dagwood made the rounds. One morning, as I sat naked in the sun doing some writing, I heard what sounded like a car coming up my driveway. All four dogs took off in a cloud of dust, barking mad. I nearly fell out of my chair, rushing back inside to grab a robe. By the time I emerged, the dogs were still barking wildly—but had, nonetheless, escorted a red SUV right up to the trailer. I stood on the porch beside the shattered remnants of the coffee mug I'd kicked over in the frenzy.

The car was so shiny. Too shiny. The starkness of it against the grainy desert landscape was jarring. As if a blood-red knife had slashed through a painting. An ink stain on a love letter.

An older gentleman's face appeared behind the descending driver's side window. I took only one step closer down onto the dirt, arms crossed, and leaned my body ever so slightly to the right as if peering around some imaginary tree. He wasn't smiling.

"Your dog was over at my place. This yellow one here." He pointed straight down at Dagwood, who stood beneath him, beaming, as if to say, *It's true! I was!*

"Oh," I said, flatly. "What was he doing?" The moment the question came out, I realized how blasé it sounded. It would probably have been best to start with one of those neighborly apologies. But he did crack a brief smile.

"Just passing through, I guess." He motioned downward at Dagwood, who was strolling back toward his favorite juniper. I watched the man's eyes as he scanned his surroundings from the safety of his car. The 1986 trailer with the rusty propane tanks. Dog toys scattered throughout the dirt like bodies on a postwar battlefield. The bag of garbage I was taking to town that day slumped against a bush. My big orange van named Bertha, immobilized and dripping transmission fluid into a catch-pan while snakeweed grew up around her thirty-five-inch tires. A chain saw resting on top of a large, dead potted plant. And a sea of panting dog faces beneath his car window. He looked disgusted. I stared down at my bare feet in the dirt.

"I'm Mike," he offered.

"Bri," I said back, holding up one hand as if we were taking attendance.

"When do you think you'll start to build?" he asked.

"I don't know," I said back, my eyes still fixed on my feet. He took the hint.

"Well I'm glad he's back. Just ... keep him on your property, okay?"

"Yes, of course, absolutely!" I said back hurriedly. The dogs and I stood perfectly still, practically in a row, as he slowly backed down the winding driveway. You have to have four-wheel drive to make a three-point turn at the top.

How dare he! I huffed, the moment he disappeared. I spun on my heel and stomped back into the trailer, knowing perfectly well that his request was beyond reasonable. I curled up on the couch, peering out the window for at least a full five minutes, just to make sure he was really gone.

The following day, I marched down to the bottom of the driveway with a shovel in one hand and a wooden post in the other. Birdie bounced along beside me, tugging at the post as if it were about to be the biggest stick I'd ever thrown for her. In front of a decent-size boulder, I dug as deep a hole as Banjo would let me. He found it much more entertaining to try to bite the shovel each time I drove it toward the ground. When I was satisfied, I jammed the post into the dirt and stepped back to admire my work: TRESPASSERS WILL BE SHOT.

Banjo stared up at me, his white snout covered in red dirt.

It had taken only a few months for me to morph into a walking caricature of "the crazy lady up on the hill." The kind the local schoolkids would have whispered about if there had been a local school. Freshly signed divorce papers, four dogs running amok, a broken-down van, a couple of pet pythons, empty wine bottles everywhere, a lawn chair on the porch, a profound sense of paranoia, and a smattering of pink plastic flamingos I had ordered off Amazon. I was also completely naked almost 100 percent of the time.

One morning I was battling with the wire legs of the flamingo that Banjo had dragged from the dirt—*again*—when I realized I hadn't seen Dagwood return from his rounds. Or perhaps I had? It wasn't uncommon for afternoons to still feel like mornings or hours to feel like days. Everything sort of blends together after a while when your day-to-day consists of wandering around alone, inventing ways to busy yourself to avoid the unwelcome company of your own thoughts. *Did Dags just crawl under his juniper earlier? Or was that yesterday?* I pondered aloud to Banjo, who looked on stoically as I undid all his hard work of unearthing the plastic bird. Standing to brush off the pebbles embedded in my knees, I shouted. *Dags?! Where you at, bubs?* I popped my head through the open trailer door to see if he had put himself back to bed, but the bed was nothing but wrinkled sheets that had arrived in the package white, but would now most certainly be considered *off*-white. Keeping any sort of bedding clean with four dogs on a desert mesa known for its flash floods and windstorms was pointless either way. I stepped back onto the deck and shaded my eyes with my hand as I scanned what I had come to call The Yard. The Yard is the two-thousand-or-so-square-foot clearing directly in front of the trailer, framed by five large junipers. Anything beyond The Yard is The Property. I divvied up The Property into sections in my mind, much like the boroughs of New York City that I grew up just forty-five-minutes outside of.

First, I scanned The Yard, which might seem obvious, but it had happened before that I'd looked right past Dagwood's sand-colored, sleeping body. He must have thought I'd lost my damn mind, calling his name from just a few dozen feet away. In his defense, most days, I too thought I'd lost my mind.

After making certain he wasn't camouflaged somewhere in plain sight, I looked down at Birdie—who was underfoot at almost all times—and shrugged. I grabbed my mug of now-tepid coffee and we took off down the driveway. Birdie and Banjo flitted side to side, bush to bush, rock to rock. Bucket walked along beside me with a lightness in her step reserved exclusively for an unexpected adventure. Our daily property strolls were usually around sunset since Dagwood always took first watch at sunrise. For absolutely no reason, I would put on one of my fanciest dresses, drown myself in ornate turquoise jewelry, pour a tall glass of wine, and say aloud to the dogs, *Children . . . let's stroll the grounds.*

Our usual route was down the driveway toward The Wash. This borough wraps around the front of The Property and is home to most all of our flowering plants. Flash floods rage through the rain-carved pathway that arcs around the entire front property line. Everything that lives in the desert survives on these violent, fleeting bouts of water. That spring, the floods had been so intense, one washed out the entire section of driveway that crossed over The Wash. Not even the two culverts buried beneath it could withstand the force of water and the whole tree trunks ripped out and carried with it along the way. When walking through the dry, relatively shallow aisle between the rock, it's hard to believe enough water could ever flow through there to do that type of damage. But it does. And it humbles me more than most anything else in my life to see it.

In the wake of such brutality, stunning tangerine-colored Indian paintbrush rises from the soil. Deep red flowers sprout from the top of the barrel cacti that cling to the patches of cryptobiotic soil beside the rocks. Firecracker penstemon, with their downturned, scarlet trumpets, crop up amid the green stalks of the yucca plants. But my favorites were the prickly pear cacti. Thick, ovular, and glowing green from such a wet spring. Bursting from nearly every inch of their waxy flesh were flowers in yellows and pinks and fuchsias and reds. Anything that blooms in the desert seems practically neon. Perhaps because there aren't many colors out there to begin with, or perhaps because their ability to bloom in the first place is just *that* triumphant. Regardless, stumbling upon a patch of phosphorescent colors anywhere in such a brown environment is akin to seeing drops of paint spilled across an otherwise blank canvas.

After squatting to take a photo of one particularly vivid orange globe mallow, I stood and hollered again, *Dagwood! C'mon, we're goin' for a walk!* I stood still, listening for the jingle of a collar, which is relatively futile when there's only a 25 percent chance that collar would be Dagwood's. After waiting a minute or so, I climbed up out of The Wash and headed north toward The Caves. The Caves is the borough that frames the northeasternmost corner of The Property. A conglomerate of massive boulders all spilled in on top of one another from the cliffs above, it is the most difficult area to navigate and therefore, the least visited. But on the hottest days, the shade between the boulders provided a kind of natural air conditioning between the rock walls and the relief of deep, cool sand. It wasn't quite hot enough in the day yet, so I wasn't surprised when Dagwood wasn't over there either. The Cracks on the west side were completely devoid of shade this time of day and decently visible from The Yard. *He's definitely not up there, it's hotter than Hades, Bucket*, I muttered as she veered off as if to head that way. By the time we got to Up Top (the final borough) I was outright annoyed. We had big plans that day to go check out what appeared to be a large, shallow puddle beneath an overhanging rock face that I had zoomed in on via satellite maps the previous day. There would most certainly be water skater bugs for Banjo to chase, and enough water for Bucket's paws to leave the ground so she could swim in her little signature circles. But it's hard to stay annoyed when you're Up Top. The way up is over the remnants of a rockslide that look much too steep to free-climb from far away, but once you get up close, it's perfectly doable. Though "perfectly doable" was not the description my mother would provide after following me up on hands and knees during her first visit to the property. "Are you fucking serious, Brianna," were her words, if I recall correctly. Once Up Top, the almost-always-snowcapped La Sal Mountains tower to the east. To the north, a row of massive sandstone fins stacked beside each other like books on a shelf. To the west, wide-open fields with one distinct dirt road slashing through toward stand-alone buttes dotting the horizon. And to the south, sixty miles of winding desert canyons and open fields right up to the base of the Abajo Mountains. Not one building, not one structure, not one person except those folks tucked in tents and trailers against the rocks just like me. On nights without any moonlight, it's so black, you can scarcely tell if you're looking out at land or sea. I don't think there's been a single day that I haven't shed a tear sitting up there. And that should speak volumes . . . because I sit up there all the time.

Up Top is my reward after surviving a day I was certain I wouldn't. Up Top is where I go to remember. Remember that I did this, I bought this. I said I would own land in the desert, and here it is. Me with my shattered heart and my broken van and my leaky trailer and my nine acres and my four dogs. One of whom was *not* Up Top. One of whom was really starting to piss me off . . .

It took a full hour for my anger to turn to worry. Perhaps that sounds surprising, but even after everything that had happened, I still think people worry too much about too much. Dags was a wanderer. Always had been. And so, it took over two hours for my worry to turn to panic. Not once, in ten years, had Dagwood been gone that long.

DAGWOOOOOOOOOD! I screamed into the midday buzz of cicadas, my lips becoming drier and more cracked with each desperate attempt. The other dogs seemed to know that the best thing they could do in this situation was stand as close to me as possible. I imagine they knew that was comforting. *He's okay*, I whispered hurriedly to Birdie, as if she were the one who was trying not to cry. Eventually, I'd yelled so much, my voice started crackling in and out. *DAG wo-od!!! DAG. WOOOOD!* Unsure what else to do, I loaded the other three into my Jeep and rolled slowly down the driveway. Once out on the road, I turned right toward the fields at the top of the mesa where I figured he'd most likely have his head buried in a hole somewhere on the scent of a kangaroo rat, or God forbid, at that neighbor's house again. I drove the dirt road one direction, then the other, then back again before deciding it was better to wait at home. *He's going to go back home, guys, he's gonna just end up going back home*, I hyperventilated aloud to Bucket, whose head was resting on my shoulder, a single string of drool sliding down my arm.

Back at the trailer, I turned the Jeep off and stared blankly out over the steering wheel. Then I pressed my forehead to it and let out one long scream. As if inebriated with grief, I stumbled from the driver's seat, collapsing to the dirt, crying so hard that no sound came out at all. It felt as though I was gasping, but air was neither coming in nor going out. Normally Bucket, Birdie, and Banjo would be howling mad to have been left in the car, but they were eerily silent. I pressed myself up to my hands and knees, trying to catch my breath.

When I lifted my head, it was his ears I saw first. I always saw his ears first. My hands flew to my mouth, hot tears dripping down over them, leaving clean streaks through otherwise dirt-covered skin. I held my breath as he approached me timidly, ears pinned back as they always were when he suspected he was in trouble. He stopped no more than a few inches from my face. I could feel his warm breath on my forehead as I lifted my eyes to meet his. And then, for the first time in my life, I screamed at him. I pounded my fists into the ground on either side of me. Spit and snot and dirt flew. *WHAT THE FUCK IS WRONG WITH YOU?! WHY DO YOU DO THIS?* I could feel something rising in my chest, something furious and ugly and long-buried. *WHY ARE YOU DOING THIS TO ME? DO YOU KNOW WHAT I DID FOR YOU?!? DO YOU KNOW WHAT I GAVE UP FOR YOU?! DO YOU KNOW WHAT PEOPLE SAY ABOUT ME?!?? DO YOU KNOW WHAT THEY DO TO ME BECAUSE OF WHAT I DID FOR YOU??! I DID THIS FOR YOU, DAGWOOD, I DID ALL OF THIS FOR YOU, I DID FUCKING EVERYTHING FOR YOU!!* I screamed, gesturing wildly at the desert around us. He stood, unflinching, unmoving as my screams reverted to sobs. I lunged forward, tossing my arms around his neck, nearly collapsing my full weight onto his fifty-five-pound body. Again, he didn't move. He didn't flinch. *I did all of this for you*, I cried, only much softer now. *You can't leave me like that, Dagwood. I need you. Please don't leave me. Please*, I begged. *I'm sorry, I'm so sorry, Dags. I'm so sorry.*

The last time I cried like that was the day he went under our tire. It was a desperate cry, a panicked cry, a cry because crying was all there was left to do. It was crippling guilt tangled up with deep despair with a seething, inseparable thread of anger woven through it all. An anger I clearly had no idea what to do with, who to hurl at, who to blame for. But as soon as I let it out, I knew I had needed to, despite how messy and ugly it all felt. Despite the fact that I'd only ever said those words aloud to someone who couldn't understand them. Or maybe he did. He waited for my screaming to stop. He waited for me to finish. Then he stepped in close and curled his head around mine, diligently licking what was left of my tears. I cupped the sides of his face and pressed my forehead to his. *We're okay*, I whispered again, correcting myself: *We're gonna be okay.*

I knelt there with my eyes closed, skin to his fur, as my breathing slowed. After a minute of complete stillness, I crawled to my feet, swiped the snot from my face with the back of my hand, and opened the Jeep for the others. They bounded out, jumping all over him, licking his mouth, playfully biting at his scruff. Clearly, he had been gone long enough to worry them too.

I'll never know where he was or why. For as much as I can read when I look into his eyes, I can't ever read it all. The slivers of chestnut, honey, and hazel around his irises look like a topographical map of desert canyons. Just as familiar. Just as unknown.

I was as torn between guilt and anger about the accident as I was about everything in my life that would follow. If Neil hadn't run Dagwood over, then there would have been no story to tell on Instagram: a story that would thrust me—by my own ignorant doing—into a limelight that would change my entire life, and ultimately ruin it. But as time went on, I knew I had to stop saying that. Because my life was not ruined by the accident. It was shattered, but not ruined. Altered, but not ruined. Devastated, but not ruined. The accident led to the exposure on Instagram, which led to continuing to work as an influencer, which led to the ability to keep running around in the desert with the dog I saved from that accident. The accident I should have told the truth about sooner. And that untruth and that limelight ultimately led to my divorce. I suppose there must have been cracks in the marriage somewhere, but they split wide open after all that. My divorce was the reason I moved to Moab, the reason I found that plot of desert so positively perfect, I still wonder if I've dreamt it. I dug myself a grave to keep my dog out of his, and what happened in the wake of that—on the surface, at least—was that my life became everything I had hoped it might. I just hadn't learned how to be happy about that yet. Because being happy felt inconsiderate. Being happy felt outright wrong. Being happy felt like I wasn't still so deeply, *deeply* sorry about how so much of it came to be.

Later that evening, I walked out onto the porch where Dagwood lay sleeping on his favorite dog bed. Climbing in behind him, I spooned my body up against his, pressing my face into his scruff, breathing in his fur. The sun was setting, the light dappling through the junipers. Our half-moon of cliffs glowed a deep pink. The ravens and the cliff swallows floated on the wind above us in what looked like a dance. We lay there watching the dusk purple melt down over it all. It was all so still, so stunning, so utterly perfect. I nestled in closer to the back of Dagwood's neck.

I did all of this for you.

chapter two

The Girl Who Hit Her Dog

I had a great time fucking your husband last night.

I sat for several minutes, staring at the email in the glow of my laptop screen, listening to my heartbeat pulsating in my ears. I was instantly slicked with sweat, as if it had come out of every single pore at once. Did you know he's already on a dating app? I took one slow deep breath and exhaled shakily. "Heidi!" I screamed. It came out like a wounded animal. It was just one month after Neil and I had separated. Just one month after I'd moved into Heidi and her husband's spare bedroom. She burst through the doorway, her socks slipping on the hardwood floor. My face must have been ghost white.

"Oh God, what's wrong? What happened?" I thrust my laptop

forward as she perched on the bed beside me. The email was short, so it only took a few seconds before she looked up at me and whispered, "Fuck."

There was no signature, no name. The email address itself was clearly fake, as if someone just smashed their fingers across a keyboard, hitting random letters and numbers. I'm sure it sounds odd, but my first thought was that the email had to have been some cruel prank coming from Neil's oldest sister. She had always despised me, and the feeling was mutual. She was a devoutly religious woman and I am *not* a devoutly religious woman, so the odds were stacked against us from the beginning. Neil had never bothered to tell his family that he hadn't considered himself religious since high school, so I was the unknowing bearer of that news when we got engaged. Fortunately, I didn't need to say much. The revelation came pretty quickly after I openly chuckled when they asked what church we'd be getting married in. His eldest sister was practically inconsolable. His brother, Stan, pulled Neil aside and urged him not to marry me. "She's not wife material," were his words.

Despite all this, everything went on as scheduled, and Neil asked Stan to be his best man. His best man at the wedding he had unabashedly condemned. There had been no change of heart. Neil hadn't demanded that he apologize to me. Stan was just handed a matching tie and directed to his place, right beside the groom. I locked eyes with him over Neil's shoulder a few times during the ceremony. The Best Man. The man who hated me, insulted me, devalued me. Standing beside the man who let him. The man I was marrying. It took me a very long time to realize how much I hated Neil for that.

Regardless, I let everything slide. I didn't want to make it worse. I didn't want to make a scene. That responsibility would fall to Neil's eldest sister several hours and several bottles of red wine later. "You're idiotic if you can't see God's glory all around us!" She stood before me, eyes glassed over, screaming at the top of her lungs, her finger pressed to the front of my champagne-pink wedding dress. It felt quite like being berated by a drifter under an overpass somewhere. In fact, I think most folks assumed she was kidding. The truth of it only sunk in when Neil's other sister was forced to drag her—still ranting—up to the car.

Neil and I didn't speak to her for a year after that. *Exactly* one year, in fact, as the text message she finally sent to Neil was to wish him a happy wedding anniversary. She said she didn't want *me* driving a wedge between them anymore. She assured him that God had forgiven her for what had happened. She just never bothered to ask if I had. And Neil hadn't either. I was expected to just shove it down, move on, keep quiet . . . because that is the kind of woman Neil's family considers "wife material."

Before Neil and I had even separated, his sister began sending all kinds of unhinged messages not only to me, but to people I worked with on Instagram. She claimed that I forced Neil to marry me by threatening to kill myself. She sent bizarre messages to a dog collar company I once worked with, telling them an unnecessarily long and sordid play-by-play of her family history. I'd never been at such a loss with how to deal with a person. I resorted to begging my father-in-law to intervene, begging him to make his daughter understand the damage she was causing for both myself and Neil. But he texted back: She's a forty-year-old woman, I can't make her do anything.

To say there was bad blood between that family and me was clearly a grievous understatement. Pretending to be someone who went on a date with Neil just to hurt me seemed on par with his sister's increasingly obsessive antics, but it still seemed grossly over the top, even for her. At the time, I couldn't imagine who else would send something like that to my personal email. Of course, I *was* a public figure on the internet. I had shared all kinds of details about my relationship and my personal life and Dagwood's accident but . . . I hadn't posted anything about Neil and I being separated. As far as followers on social media knew, I had just been down in Moab for a few weeks instead of Salt Lake City where Neil and I had been living.

I sat up and looked at Heidi. "Maybe he *is* on a dating app . . ." I said, trying to hold back tears. My face was already salted over from the ones I would cry religiously each morning upon waking to find this was all still happening.

Heidi opened her phone, typing furiously as I held my breath. I watched her shoulders drop, her face change. I can only describe it as disappointment. None of the people who knew Neil wanted to believe this was happening either. I lunged for the phone with one hand, using my T-shirt to dry my eyes as I leaned in closer to the screen. The main photo was one taken on a professional photoshoot we had done for an outdoor brand almost three years prior. He was wearing a puffy coat, smiling up at Dagwood, who was draped across his shoulders, tongue flapping. Heidi leaned over my shoulder. "He literally doesn't even look like that anymore . . ."

I whipped around to face her. "Heidi, anyone could have screenshotted this photo, it's been on the internet since 2017. They could be faking this whole thing . . . catfishing someone or whatever it's called," I said excitedly. She stared back at me, expressionless. I continued scrolling. "Look, see! These are all photos from my Instagram page, anyone could have— Oh my God . . ." I interrupted myself when I saw the next photo. It was us. A wide shot of Neil and I holding hands, jumping off a sandstone cliff together into the inky green water of Lake Powell. That day had been beautiful. One of my favorites, in fact. Back then, we were still invincible. I thrust the phone into Heidi's face. "See! You think someone is gonna use a photo of him and his *wife* on their dating profile?! I mean that's ridic—"

"Bri," she cut me off, "see this thing here?" Her finger hovered over a blue checkmark next to Neil's full name. "This is, like, the same thing as Instagram. It's the same thing you have. A blue checkmark means he's verified. To get that on this app, you literally have to submit, like, photo identification. My friend just did it a few months ago, so I just . . ." She trailed off. But I refused to believe it. I couldn't let myself believe it. We had been together for eleven years. I had barely been gone one month. I had already gotten that email . . . this had to be the same person pulling this bizarre ruse.

"I think you should call him, Heidi," I said urgently. She took a deep breath as if about to protest. "I really don't think it's him. None of the writing even sounds like him. And if it's not him, he deserves to know that someone is out here impersonating him, don't you think?!" I shouted after her as she stood from the bed, pausing to look back at me from the bedroom door. To protect him was still my instinct.

"Stay. Here," she said firmly. "I'll text him."

I never knew how much time passed between events anymore. She may have come back two minutes later or two hours. If my memory was sharp enough, it would surely have killed me. I leapt from the bed the moment I heard her hand on the knob. But I knew before she even spoke.

"It's his profile, Bri." She couldn't seem to bring herself to meet my eyes. "But he said he didn't sleep with anybody, so that email . . . he didn't know. I'm so sorry." I collapsed back onto the bed, pressing my face to the top of Dagwood's head.

No no no no no, I whispered. Methodically, I stood up to pull the curtains closed on the windows, still chanting *no no no no no* . . . . Heidi stood in the doorway as I climbed back into bed. She had started to cry too. Bucket curled up in between my legs beneath the covers, her head resting on my thigh. Dagwood and Birdie lay with their backs pressed against mine. "Shut the lights off." My voice was completely monotone. "And shut the door, too," I said as she turned to leave. Prior to this, there was a strict open-door policy. I'd been on the phone with a suicide hotline twice that week. Heidi didn't know what else to do. She hadn't expected her spare bedroom to become some sort of asylum. Regardless, she sighed and gently shut the door behind her. A minute later, I shot up and called out her name. "Heidi!" She flung the door open immediately. I don't think she had stepped away to begin with.

"Heidi . . . can you just . . ." I sniffled, my voice cracking, "can you ask him to take down the picture of us?"

Despite having that blue checkmark of my own, despite being the official "verified" version of myself with over 250,000 followers on Instagram . . . it hadn't ever really occurred to me that anyone would consider me "famous." Famous people, to me, were Beyoncé and Kim Kardashian and Leonardo DiCaprio. I was just a woman who wrote stories and posted photos of dogs to an app on my phone. Why would anyone be so invested in my marriage that they would insert themselves into it? Over the next week or two, it finally sunk in that people on the internet no longer saw me the way I saw myself. It started with the messages.

Where's your husband?
Did you move?
Did you see what Neil's sister commented on your photo?
Is Bertha broken down, why are you staying at Heidi's?
How come we haven't seen your hubby in a while?
Where's Neil?
Where's your husband?
Where's your husband?
Where's your husband?

Then people started tagging their friends under old posts of mine, old photos of Neil and me with our arms wrapped around each other, laughing or kissing or leaning out of Bertha's bright orange front window. Photos I wouldn't have dared look at if they hadn't been waiting there in my notifications like land mines.

@I haven't seen the husband in a while do you think they split?!
@ No! OMG Amy, do you think?? I'm devastated . . .

YOU'RE devastated? How the fuck do you think I feel!? I typed back furiously into my phone one afternoon, my thumb hovering over the send button before deleting the message and closing the app. I'm not sure who they thought was on the other side of their screen. I had no assistant, no social media manager, no buffer between me and all those thousands of people. It's surreal to slowly watch yourself become a fictional character, a two-dimensional image that exists only inside an app. Especially when I'd made it my mission to try to be as transparent and genuine as possible. Apparently, I was one of those naïve ones who thought that's what social media was for in the first place. I wanted so badly to convey my humanness, to try to use it as a point of connection. And yet, even after all that, I found myself surrounded by people who were talking about me as though I wasn't right there . . . as though they had tapped me on the shoulder to get my attention, then spoke directly through me. I could never have predicted that being seen by so many people would be the loneliest I would ever feel.

I can't remember exactly when Heidi told me about Reddit, but I remember her sitting on the edge of my bed, holding my hand, as if about to deliver a diagnosis. Reddit was a website I had heard of but didn't know much about. Its founders describe it as "a discussion website." It's a social-media-type platform with more than fifty million users who primarily share content from elsewhere in order to create discussions about said content. Reddit itself is divided into "subreddits" based on these different discussion topics. Each subreddit comes up with its own introduction and set of posting rules prominently displayed. The subreddit has "moderators" to enforce those rules, which is a volunteer position, usually taken on by the person who started the subreddit to begin with. Rules can be things like "No more jokes about suicide, but feel free to talk about how ugly she is." In short, Reddit is the self-governed, depraved Wild West of the internet.

I felt geriatric as Heidi attempted to explain what sounded like a different language to me. Finally, she just threw her hands up. "There's one about you . . . about us, a bunch of us influencers in the outdoor industry. Apparently, it's a snark page." I stared blankly at her. "What the fuck is a snark page?"

Years later, a *TIME* magazine article would describe the phenomenon of snark subreddits as "pages which exist for popular TikTokers, wives of major celebrities, YouTubers, and other public figures, that are meant to foster a community of like-minded people who dislike that particular person or group of famous people and feel a responsibility to shed light on unsavory ways in which they believe they are using their platforms." A "community." A "community" of "like-minded" people. People who gather together with one single thing in common: the hatred of a complete stranger. Never in my wildest dreams could I have imagined that I'd be one of those strangers . . . that I'd have my very own sub-reddit called "MadiaSnark." The first few things I read about my-self pertained to Dagwood's accident. What really happened to Dagwood? Where did all that GoFundMe money really go? The rest were about my marriage. Petty, middle school gossip. Who left who and who said what. It sunk in slowly that this was a public discussion board about the very things I'd cried to an operator on a suicide hotline about the night before. A screenshot of my irate response to the email about Neil's dating profile was prominently displayed. It had been some stranger on this page who had sent it. Someone baiting a response from me so that they could all laugh about it together.

I should have stopped scrolling. But I didn't. I couldn't. The com-ments about me were vicious. I could barely see the screen through my tears. Everyone was in agreement that Neil and I "had definitely split" and that he had "definitely left me." I understood why they wanted to believe that. It's much more comfortable to believe the quiet one in the relationship is as sweet and perfect as they appear to be. The loud ones, the bold ones, especially the women . . . they're much easier to hate. They're much easier to blame. The reality was, Neil and I left each other. I'd left just recently. He'd left a long time ago.

"Maybe you should post some sort of statement that you guys are no longer together? Just put it to rest so they stop asking?" A friend suggested this to me on the phone a few days after I'd discovered the subreddit. "What is this, a goddamn tabloid mag-azine? What am I supposed to say?" I shouted. "That Neil is an alcoholic? That I had no idea how bad things had gotten? That Dagwood's accident destroyed us? Should I tell everyone that sometimes this app I'm still talking to them on feels like it's ruined my fucking life? Do you think that's what I should say?" I breathed heavily, angrily into the phone. In her softest voice, she whispered, "I'm sorry, Bri. I know you didn't expect it to end up like this . . . but it did. Just ask people to respect your privacy or something." But I had already learned that people like me were no longer awarded the luxury of privacy.

These two things—the accident, the separation—they were so knotted up together in ways I couldn't untie. But the accident had already happened. It had happened almost two years ago by then. No longer being with Neil was still practically news to *me*. I felt exactly like I had in the midst of everything that happened to Dagwood. I just couldn't tell the truth. That would make it real.

Instead, I opened Instagram and posted a long letter to over a quarter of a million people about the truth I *was* ready to tell.

It was us, I wrote. We were driving the car that hit Dagwood.

Saying "we" was my idea of a public peace offering. If Neil saw it, if his family saw it, I wanted them to know it was still my intention to protect him. It's so hard to shut that off when you loved someone for that long. I didn't blame him. I've never blamed him. But two people can't be behind the steering wheel of one car.

chapter three

Never-Never Land

There's an arm draped over my waist, the hand hanging limp on the sheet beside me. A strong hand. A calloused hand. A construction worker hand. The hair on this wrist is so blond, it's nearly white. A smattering of deep-brown freckles extends clear down to the fingertips. This is not my husband's hand. I've cheated on my husband . . .

Through my foggy, still-slightly-drunk vision, I make eye contact with Bucket across the room. Below her powdered-sugar-white eyebrows, her eyes shine a glossy blue. Those old-dog eyes that have seen all kinds of things. My forehead flushes with sweat, I can feel my heart beating in my stomach, churning up a sickness that requires every muscle in my body to keep it down. I lurch toward the side of the mattress, fumbling for my phone. The searing light of the screen reveals a handful of missed messages. Where are you? Did you leave with that guy? There are no messages from my husband. It's only then that I remember that I don't have a husband anymore.

This routine took place most every morning. I'd wake up—usually hungover—and spend the first few minutes reminding myself where I was, and who I was, and what I was. *My name is Brianna Madia. I am a thirty-year-old "Instagram influencer." I'm living in a small bedroom I'm renting from a friend in Moab, Utah. I have three dogs, two ball pythons, and one soon-to-be-ex-husband.* This is who I am now. This realization hits me every morning like a freight train. It hits me every morning as if I'm realizing it for the very first time. But there was no better place to flee from reality than Moab, Utah.

If a movie is set on Mars, there's a high likelihood it was filmed in Moab. This is fitting, of course, since moving there was more akin to leaving the planet. Geographically, Moab is a vast expanse of red rock formations and extensive canyons, mesas, and buttes carved out over time by the waters of the Colorado and the Green Rivers. Tourists flock there to see Canyonlands and Arches National Park, and Dead Horse Point where the famous final scene of *Thelma and Louise* was filmed. Outdoorspeople come to camp and mountain bike and rock climb and trail run and rappel through narrow sandstone slot canyons . . . oftentimes all in one day. The stunning, seemingly endless sedimentary rock is referred to by experts as "layer cake geology." Layers and layers of different textures and types all melted on top of each other, as if someone sliced through billions of years of history with one big, sharp knife.

Demographically, an estimated three to four million tourists visit Moab each year, but only about five thousand people *actually* live there. These residents fall into a small handful of categories that I invented when I moved there in May of 2020. Not only had my world changed drastically, but the entire planet too. It was the early stages of COVID-19, the global pandemic that would go on to kill more than six million people. When governments began confining everyone to their homes, photos of some of the most densely populated areas on the planet began circulating online. Empty lawns framing the Eiffel Tower. Times Square abandoned. Shibuya Street Crossing in Tokyo—where an average 2.4 million people shuffled through each day—completely devoid of life. People began stockpiling food, clearing supermarket shelves of toilet paper, fist fighting in the aisles of their local Walmart. Some folks were buying up every Clorox wipe, every bottle of Purell they could find to sell on the internet at significantly higher prices. It was like living in a sci-fi movie.

Regardless, with those travel bans in place, Moab became its own little bubble. No one in and no one out. So it was much easier to categorize the characters in my plot without all those tourists milling about. I should mention that this is about the time I started turning everything that was happening to me into a fictional story. Because those seemed much easier to survive. People can't hurt you if they're just characters. Bad decisions are just a part of the plotline. And a plotline is the perfect way to trick yourself into believing you have a say in how it's all going to end. If nothing is *really* real, then nothing really matters. A brilliant defense mechanism, I thought. My therapist agreed, only she called it by its clinical name: disassociation.

Now, anyone who lives in Moab can surely call themselves

"a local," but when I hear the word, it's the *real* locals who come to mind. The born-and-raised-and-never-left locals. The blue-collar-through-and-through, rough-around-the-edges locals. Before the tourism boom, the only real work to be had in Moab was in the uranium mines, and that wasn't as long ago as it might sound. Some of those folks didn't like all the tourists and the new rules that came along with them. Some idiot in a rental Jeep would roll off a cliff, causing the county to close a road that locals had been driving for thirty-plus years, no problem. A friend of mine was born there in the seventies and hadn't lived a day elsewhere in his life. "You could camp wherever you wanted when I was growin' up," he'd regale me. "You could pitch a tent right under Delicate Arch and ain't nobody'd give a shit!" I would not take his word on this, but if you ever find yourself at Woody's Tavern on a Thursday night, feel free to ask him yourself.

Besides spoiling the fun, the tourists crowded the trails and raised the prices of absolutely everything. Moab is the first and last town on a long stretch of desert highway, so you've got no choice but to pay what they're charging you. The town benefited financially, of course. Some folks far more than others. All those tourists needed places to stay, so construction companies made a killing spitting out one hotel after another. Rental companies and rich people from out of town swept the real estate market to create their absurdly priced Airbnbs. All those tourists needed to be fed and guided and entertained too, but those industries were hardly as lucrative.

This is where the circus people come in. I refer to these folks as "the circus people" not in a derogatory way, but purely because I don't quite know how else to describe them. A gaggle of beautiful, talented athletes and extreme-sports enthusiasts with rippling muscles and a combined body fat index of 8 percent. They hang from thirty-foot silk sheets doing acro-yoga in midair. They land on top of desert towers in the middle of nowhere via some guy's personal helicopter. They rig up rope swings that send them into three-hundred-foot free falls between two narrow canyon walls. They're skydivers and rock climbers and photographers and fire spinners and mountain bikers and BASE jumpers and whitewater kayakers and slackliners. Some are permanent transplants from other states, some are just guiding there for the season, and some are transients whose vans broke down so they just decided to stay and get a job waiting tables.

Moab is the island of misfit toys. It's Never-Never Land. It's a small town full of *big* personalities. Main Street is always rife with some of the most outrageous off-roading, Mad-Max-looking vehicles you'll ever see, and odds are, whoever owns them probably lives in them. Every week, without fail, word spreads about some ketamine-fueled rave taking place out in the middle of nowhere. Skydivers will drop in to the party from passing planes above; their parachutes floating down through the elaborate light show, glowing like neon army men tossed down by a child. They live in a small, never-ending Burning Man.

The true drug of choice in Moab, however, is adrenaline. A guy I slept with for a little while used to wake up at five o'clock in the morning, kiss me on the forehead, and go jump off a cliff. With a parachute of course, but regardless, BASE jumping was as much a part of his routine as getting up and letting the dogs out or listening to NPR is for me. Andy and I met when he followed me into the bathroom at a party and asked *me* if he could ask *his girlfriend* if he and I could hang out sometime. I stared back, dumbfounded, convinced now that I truly had moved to a different planet. *Who the hell are these people? What the fuck is going on?* He went on to say that he and his girlfriend were testing out being in an open relationship, and apparently, I was the lucky recipient of this once-in-a-lifetime opportunity. Realistically, I was just the "new girl" and, therefore, one of few women left in the entire town who didn't despise him. Still slightly stunned, I punched my number into his phone. "I'll let you know what she says," he said, excitedly, as if he was going to go ask his mom if we could have a sleepover.

"I mean, who am I to judge?" I said to my mom on the phone the next day. "At least they're not lying to each other. I was married to a guy who couldn't even manage that."

"Maybe just sleeping with someone with no strings attached would be a good way for you to get back out there, Brianna," she said. (If you're finding it strange that this conversation is taking place with my mother, you wouldn't be the first. But my mother and I tell each other everything and I mean *everything*.) However, it's hard to picture yourself "getting back out there" when you were never really "out there" to begin with. I had been with one person from age nineteen to thirty. That was one-third of my entire life. I had watched all my friends back East go through their twenties—the quintessential dating years—from the comfort of a partner's arms. The awkward first dates, the awkward last dates, the cheesy pickup lines, the Tinder profiles, the late-night hookups . . . The things I never *ever* would have imagined I would have to do someday. In fact, by the time I found myself in that position, all those friends were married. Many of them even had children. I became a bit of a left fielder in our group chat. They would send photos of their babies learning to swim, and I'd reply, So cute!! Also, you guys, I slept with a 22-year-old raft guide last night. One time I sent a drunken text to them at midnight, which was two o'clock in the morning on the East Coast. Ali replied immediately, which surprised me. Ali you're up?? Wht are yo doingup? I typed into the phone with one eye closed. Breastfeeding! she texted back. But entertain me, what happened tonight?!

I was cramming my entire twenties into my thirtieth year of life. I was trying to pretend it was fun.

Besides the raft guide and the BASE jumper, there were others. The guy from Texas. The construction worker with the long blond dreadlocks. The semipro mountain biker who later told his friends that he "had always wanted to fuck an influencer." Perhaps even stranger than the lineup of men was the fact that my dogs tagged along on every date. One guy invited me to Colorado for a night, and ended up driving with Birdie on his lap. The cab of his pickup barely held us all. I'd wake up in bed with a man I didn't really know on one side, and the dog I'd known forever on the other. After all, Bucket *had* to sleep in bed with me no matter where we found ourselves. I figured I was going to have to date *a lot* before it would ever feel even remotely normal. And I was flattered how fast they fell for me. I was flattered that one of them looked into my eyes and told me he loved me after only two weeks. I stared back, smirking, shaking my head. "I don't even think you know what that means, Andy."

I did *like* some of them. But I liked all of them better as soon as they left. Because, deep down, it was only the idea of them that I was interested in. And whether or not they knew it, it was only the idea of me that they were "in love" with. None of them ever got to see who I *really* was, I made sure of that. Or perhaps it's just hard to show anyone who you are when you've lost yourself entirely.

chapter four

Manic

I am lying on the floor of a room my friend Gina is renting. Heidi kicked me out of the room I was renting from her just a few days ago. She and her husband said they couldn't help me anymore. It wasn't that they didn't want to. They just didn't know how. And they were less than enthused with a shirtless, dread-headed construction worker sneaking out in the morning.

So I packed up my three dogs and four bags and moved back into my van in late July of 2020, when the average high was ninety-six degrees. My two snakes needed electricity for their heat lamps, so I begged my friends-cum-landlords to let me keep their tanks plugged in to their garage until I could find a place for them. My van, Bertha, had no source of temperature control whatsoever, meaning it was near impossible to be inside of her for more than ten minutes without boiling to death. So technically, I wasn't really *living* anywhere.

On this particular morning, however, I found myself on an inflatable sleeping pad on the concrete floor beside the bed where Gina and her boyfriend slept. We had only met a few weeks before, but she immediately designated herself my caretaker. I was more of a project than a person at that point. I stared up at her hand hanging off the mattress above me. I could feel my heart beating in my forehead. My lips were so chapped, they had begun to bleed at the corners. When I stood to find the bathroom, I screamed out in pain, startling the two of them awake. Collapsing back to the ground, I held my left foot up in the air. It felt like it weighed twenty pounds. With my eyes closed and my back pressed to the cold concrete, I listened as they told me what happened. I'd been dropped off at around six o'clock in the morning, wearing nothing but a bikini, by someone they didn't know. They said I had all three dogs, no shoes, and a deep, bloody hole in the bottom of my foot as wide as a dime. And then I remembered.

The day prior, I had been sitting on the side of the Colorado River, attempting to have a quiet afternoon wherein I might actually be forced to sit with my own thoughts. I knew I would have to eventually. But apparently, today was not that day. Out of nowhere, I heard heavy bass in the distance. The dogs lifted their heads toward the sound. Around the wide and winding corner of the river, a party barge of at least fifteen rafts, thirty or more paddleboards, and a countless number of gigantic inflatable pool floats emerged. As they got closer, I realized they had built an entire DJ booth with four-foot speakers on either side. It was mounted to a metal frame across an inflatable fifteen-foot raft, and they were floating directly toward us. Someone from the crowd yelled out, "Hey it's Bucket and Dagwood . . . and Birdie!" They were often recognized before I was.

Within a matter of minutes, a full-blown rave had cropped up on the beach that was previously vacant. I recognized a few people, but not the guy in the top hat who gently placed a tab of acid onto my tongue. I don't remember much, but I know I spun around dancing and wandering through the sand for at least the next eight hours. Everyone had brought tents and camping gear and warm clothes, but I hadn't even planned on being there in the first place. I had nothing but a bathing suit, a wet pair of jean shorts, a water bottle, and three dogs. The only clear memory I have of that night was limping around, freezing cold, looking for something—anything—to lie under. The music had finally stopped. The silence felt so much lonelier. It must have been almost three o'clock in the morning by the time I crawled inside a large, collapsed beach umbrella that had fallen over on its side. I lifted one half like a clam shell and climbed in. Bucket, Dagwood, and Birdie funneled in one by one, curling up all around me, filling up every inch of space between us with their soft fur and warm breath. I lay with my head on the cold sand, my arms around the dogs, shivering, looking up at the stars. They were so bright, it hardly seemed like a night sky at all. I took one sand-covered hand, cupped it to my mouth, and cried.

The next morning, I had no recollection of what exactly happened to my foot, but it was apparent that I had stepped on something very big and very sharp. "You were like, covered in blood," Gina said, wide-eyed. I lifted my eyes to meet hers. She reached out, patting my head, like some sort of sad dog. "I slept in an umbrella," I mumbled.

When my psychiatrist said the words "manic episode," a certain image came to mind. I envisioned it being something that would come on suddenly but obviously, like a seizure or a panic attack. You'd know *immediately* that something was very wrong. Perhaps you'd spend a few hours crouched in a corner, debilitated, hallucinating, throwing things, rocking back and forth. Whatever it was, it seemed like something that would most certainly ruin your day. So you could imagine my surprise when she told me I'd likely been experiencing one for over two months at that point. Given what I *thought* I knew about that condition, I protested. "I'm really depressed and really fucked up, Robin, but that's like . . ."

"Brianna, you're practically textbook," she interrupted, reaching for some sort of actual textbook. I had propped my cell phone up against a water bottle on the coffee table beside the couch so I didn't have to get up for our FaceTime call. "Is that like . . . bipolar?" I asked. My breathing grew heavy. I was trying not to cry, but I cried every day. I cried all the time, about everything. When I wasn't crying or sleeping, I was going BASE jumping or climbing into the back of a pickup truck with a bunch of strangers offering to take me to a rave somewhere where we'd all run around naked. Whenever I *did* sleep, it was usually because I had drank myself there. From one day to the next, I didn't know whether I was on top of the world or drowning at sea. Sometimes it felt like everything was falling into place, which would be a stark departure from the night before when everything was falling apart. Despite eating less than two hundred calories every other day, I had boundless energy. I'd come up with all sorts of grand ideas. *A YouTube channel! Or maybe a clothing collaboration or a writing retreat? I could move back up to Salt Lake City. I could drive over to Grand Junction to buy a gun and end all of this. I'm gonna look up the cost of a skydiving license. Technically I could move to Mexico. Technically I could do whatever I want!* I was like a schoolkid pulling things out of a hat on career day.

I abruptly shot up from an air mattress on a different floor one morning, and exclaimed to the dogs, *Let's look at some property, shall we, kiddos?* They were always the first to hear about all of my brilliant ideas. I scrolled through local real estate websites—all two of them—for lot listings. When I set the price filter, there were fewer than five left. Twenty-eight acres in La Sal with the bones of a burnt-down barn still visible. A three-acre lot smashed between two new RV parks near the center of town. I scrolled back up to the ranch. It was high enough in elevation to start looking more mountainous and less desert-y. *I bet it gets wayyy colder up there in the winters too*, I said to Bucket, who was already lying in the square patch of sun streaming through the window.

The next two listings were just pictures of red squares drawn on satellite images. Two nondescript patches of dirt in the middle of other dirt. Who divided this weirdly wide-open field? It would be like cutting a slightly sideways square-shaped slice from the middle of a sheet cake. I want *this* very piece right here! It's not even like there were toppings. The plots were nothing but dirt. Nary a plant higher than your knee.

I don't recall what the final listing was, as I was too fixated on how random the last two were. Reluctantly, I increased the budget and hit refresh. Seven listings now. I could tell immediately from the aerial photo that one of them was in town. The final listing had a picture of a gigantic wall of rocks. I clicked it, thrilled that there was something to look at besides dirt. It felt like my heart rate slowed with each picture I scrolled through. Photo after photo after photo. The picture quality was nothing to write home about, of course, but it seemed kind of fitting for selling a nine-acre plot of untamed desert. There were dozens and dozens of juniper trees. Big ones. They had to be at least two hundred years old. A thirty-foot rock wall cradled the whole back side, as if the land were tucked in the crook of its arm. A sandy wash wrapped around the front beside the road. It looked like a moat. The last photo was an aerial view with black dashes denoting the latitude and longitude of the property lines. I zoomed out on the map. The land sat directly atop a mesa that overlooked what appeared to be absolutely nothing. Like looking out from the window of a tower. I picked up my phone and dialed the number across the top of the website.

It took me nothing more than rounding the corner for the Realtor to know I was going to buy it. Oddly, it had been on the market for eight years. I made her promise it wasn't some sort of haunted burial ground. I couldn't *imagine* why it had just sat here all those years. It was owned by a couple who lived in Salt Lake City. Or California maybe. They bought it. Or maybe they inherited it. (These are the kinds of details a manic person can't always hold on to.) Why they had it, who knows. They didn't want it anymore, and that's all I cared about.

Over the next few days, I pulled together tax records and background information from the past six years of my life—which, by the way, is more complicated than it sounds when half of those years were spent living in a van and the other half were spent living in six different apartments, spare rooms, or houses packed with five grown adults who get *a lot* of mail. Not to mention that my Instagram income was such that I had about 150 different W-2s each year from various companies I'd worked with. Even if they sent me five hundred dollars and a sweatshirt, I still had to provide a W9. But technically, I was still "self-employed," which translates to loan companies as "poor." (Although in professional negotiations, they use the term "high risk.") I heard this a lot during the hours I spent on the phone with various banks and credit unions and lending companies. I was frantic. It was all I thought about every second of the day. I had piles of paper and lists and Post-its spread across my favorite table at the public library like I'd been working a cold case for twenty years. I begged, and I mean *begged* every person I managed to get on the phone. Most of them sounded genuinely sincere when they said they wished they could help. "I'm so sorry. You just didn't qualify." "We used to give out lot loans, but we don't anymore, I'm sorry." "Our interest rates have changed because of COVID." It was always something. There was always some hurdle, some catch at the end of each phone call. A man named Phillip from a small loan company out of Rochester, New York, started in on the sentence I'd assumed was coming. "We'd love to work with you but we only give lot loans if you can put down 50 percent in cash up front."

I sat straight up in my chair as if shocked by a live wire. "I can do that," I said hurriedly. "What is that, that's . . ." I shuffled the papers around frantically on the desk. My Realtor had said I should go ten below asking, and I had enthusiastically nodded my head, feeling very grown up because I understood these real estate words. "Okay, so if they accept, that's . . . it will be . . . half down would only be $60,000!" I screamed as if someone had just told me I had *won* $60,000. ("Only $60,000" is another absurd thing one might say whilst steeped in the make-believe world of complete and total mania, by the way.)

If I took every single penny out of my checking and my savings accounts and used everything I had in the retirement account from my old nine-to-five, I'd be just under ten grand short. Asking anyone in my family to borrow money was off the table. I refused. Though, none of them were in a position to be loaning out money anyway. Maybe my dad was. Maybe he could make everything up to me by writing me a check, like one of those WASPy East Coast kids I had despised so much. I was dead set on buying that land, but I was even more dead set on making sure I never owed my father a goddamn thing for it.

I waited two weeks for one more check to clear. Then I sold the Jeep I'd had since high school for the last six thousand dollars

I needed to have just enough and not a penny more. At seventeen, I'd thrown a fit when my mother showed up with a used sedan for me to drive. I was so adamant that I "would never drive a car like that," that she went and traded it out for that used Jeep Wrangler, threw the keys across the room at me, slammed her door, and didn't speak to me for days.

The older I got, the farther away I got, the more I began to despise that materialistic world and the kind of person it almost made me. I was so guilty about demanding that Jeep that I'd kept it all those years. I held on to it for thirteen years, despite it sitting immobile in a dirt lot behind Neil's office for the past five. I held on to it, and I really had no idea why.

It felt positively poetic to have that piece of my past be the final thing to go. Traded out for the last few thousand dollars of a dream. A dream I wouldn't have even thought to dream when I climbed behind the wheel of that car half my life ago. When I finally got the check, I texted a photo of it to my mother. She had always felt guilty about not making enough money to help her kids out with big life things like this. Good thing I had the Jeep, mom, I wrote. Thank you.

Once I secured the loan, the sellers accepted my offer immediately. Ten below asking. Turned out it had been in my price range after all. After signing about four hundred papers I didn't really read, and agreeing to a loan whose 12 percent interest rate I didn't really register, my Realtor handed me a big folder with all the copies of my paperwork inside. It had a white picket fence across the front of it.

And just like that, I had done it. I had frantically, unexpectedly, and recklessly done it, but I'd done it.

Buying land in the desert was my dream. But before that, it had been *our* dream. Mine and Neil's. *We* were going to buy land and build the house of *our* dreams. *Us.* Since I was nineteen, everything had been *us* and *we* and *our*. It's shocking how deeply ingrained those words are in your vocabulary after so many years.

I accomplished the dream on my own, but the reasons were different than I imagined. I had pictured me and Neil popping champagne outside a title office one day, sitting in the van drawing up ramshackle sketches of what our house might look like, which juniper we'd build it next to. I'd just bounce from one desert-dust-covered fairy tale to the next. But all I could see now when I looked at that land was a really good place to hide. A beautiful tower to banish myself to. After all, according to Neil and his family and the incessant commentary from strangers on the internet . . . I was the villain. To be cast out was what I deserved. Up there, I would be safe from all the villagers and their torches. The mania and the depression . . . it was starting to feel like a terminal illness, anyway. And I just wanted to die in peace.

chapter five

The Bite Mark

One sunny afternoon, I went for a walk with Aubrey, who was a friend of Gina's. At the time, she was living in her van following her own divorce, so we had been linked up on some sad first date since being sad was what we had in common. But she also had a dog, so we had that in common too. Hank leapt out of her van and barreled toward my pack. Now, if you took Dagwood, doubled his weight and size, and toasted his fur just a bit more golden-brown, you'd have Hank. This drastic size difference only became apparent to me a short while later, when I had my legs wrapped around his back from behind, my two hands bloodied and punctured, trying desperately to pry his jaws off of Dagwood's face.

We wrestled on the ground, Aubrey standing there motionless, her hands pressed to the sides of her face. I couldn't really blame her. I used to be the one who froze in harrowing situations, but that changes once you get used to having no one else there to step in. Hank opened his mouth ever so slightly and bit down again, just about an inch from Dagwood's eyeball. That's when I started screaming. Bracing my foot against the trunk of the juniper tree we were rolling around next to, I jammed my hands as far down Hank's throat as I could, and pulled his jaws apart. I felt nothing as one of his teeth crunched down on the knuckle of my right ring finger. I still feel nothing there today. Nerve damage, the doctor said. But that knuckle created enough of a gap for Dagwood to pull his head out. As he stumbled backward, Hank lunged forward once more and tore a flap of flesh from Dagwood's front leg. Aubrey finally jumped in, grabbing Hank's collar as I crawled frantically toward Dagwood. There was so much dust kicked up in the scuffle that it floated down around us like snow, sticking to the bright red blood slicking the top of Dagwood's head.

I don't remember much of what came immediately after. I know Aubrey was horrified, hysterical, apologetic. I know I called out to her as I carried Dagwood to my car. "It's okay, Aubrey! It wasn't your fault!" Despite my beloved dog bleeding in my arms because of hers, despite the trauma of seeing Dagwood, once again, on an exam table at the hospital, I wasn't angry with her. I even shouldered the medical bills because I just couldn't bring myself to ask her to. I didn't want to make her feel as though she was to blame for an accident. If she was anything like me, she would blame herself enough already.

Ultimately, Dagwood only had superficial wounds. He needed seventeen stitches, which they administered as I sat out in the waiting room. "Do *you* need medical attention?" the receptionist asked, peering her head around the desk. I looked down at the blood dripping onto the linoleum floor. I guess I had just assumed it was Dagwood's. There were four decent wounds on my hand, three on the fingers, and one in the soft skin between my thumb and pointer. Almost exactly one year prior, I had stared down at a different bite in this very place, on this very hand. The teeth had punctured just enough to leave clear, red teeth marks, with bruised purple half-moons above each . . . but not enough to break the skin. I figured this was something the police would take into account if I called them. But I wouldn't have dared call them. After all, Neil had never done anything like that before, and as I sat there on the floor, hugging my knees, tucked beside the refrigerator, I assured myself he would never do anything like that again. He was drunk. We both were.

Don't waste their time, Brianna, I thought to myself . . . *you'll ruin their Christmas.*

I was still pressed to the side of the fridge when I heard more glass break as the coffee table flipped over with a loud thud. Dog paws frantically scrambled across the hardwood floor as I stood to run to the living room. But seconds later, I heard the garage door opening. I got to the window just in time to see it closing behind him. Sprinting outside, I banged my fists against the metal, screaming, sobbing, pleading with him . . . begging him not to do what I thought he was about to do.

He went away the next day. I was only allowed to come in for a one-hour visit later that week, so I stood in the sterile room, nervously clutching a Yahtzee box to my chest. It was a game we loved playing together. A nurse came in first, guiding him to a stiff leather chair across from mine. Our eyes met for the first time, but only because I was looking at them . . . not because they were actually there. In his hand, he held one powdered jelly donut hole. I could see remnants of the previous ones around the edges of his mouth. With encouragement, he finally began speaking, rather, not so much speaking, but listing. A bullet point timeline of all the lies he'd been telling for the last six months. Lies about how many beers he'd *actually* had, lies about where the money had gone, where the dented front bumper on the truck had come from, why he couldn't keep his food down, why he was up at all hours of the night, why he always locked the door to the room in the basement where he played guitar . . .

All the while, I stared straight down at my knees, my fingers tightening around the worn, red edges of the box until my knuckles were white. It wasn't like having the rug ripped out from under me. It was like having the rug and the floor and the entire earth on which it existed ripped out. He had come there to pull the pin on a grenade.

I had come there to play Yahtzee.

That very night, I booked a flight back to Connecticut to be with my mom. I was in shock. I needed her. She was my best friend, and the only other person in my world who knew what it was like to be married to an addict. Neil's family was outraged that I would leave.

They said I abandoned him, that I was a bad wife, that perhaps I was even the cause of his drinking in the first place. "She drove him to drink!" I believe the misogynistic old saying goes.

Despite his family's ever-increasing attempts to drive us apart, Neil and I tried to make it work. When I got back to Utah, there was therapy and support groups and workbooks and weekly check-ins. We had ten whole years to try to salvage, after all. I didn't want to be alone. But it turns out, being with an addict was the most alone I would ever feel. Having to tell someone what they did, what they said, how many glasses they broke, how many lies they told. After a while, I started to question if they even counted as lies. Can something *be* a lie if the memory of it truly doesn't exist within that person? They're not choosing to ignore it or pretending it didn't happen. In Neil's brain, it quite literally *didn't*. I wasn't alone in those moments. He was right there, right there in front of me. We both had to live through it . . . but only I had to live *with* it. Even years later, even stone-cold sober, those memories exist only in me, because they never even formed in him.

I learned that in one of the final support group meetings I went to. We sat side by side among all the other war-torn couples, the desperate parents clutching the hands of their children with scabbed faces and sunken eyes. A video was playing on a projector that looked like the one from my high school health class. In it, a neurologist explained—in layman's terms—what happens to an addict's brain, how memories don't form. How it takes a minimum of nine months of complete sobriety for the brain to even *begin* to resume normal function.

I couldn't breathe in that room. I had to get out of that room. When we got home that night, I locked myself in the downstairs bathroom with a half-empty bottle of red wine I'd hidden behind the pipes under the sink. I'm sure that sounds absurd . . . to listen to a neurologist describing your husband's mashed potato brain and then go home and cope by using the very thing that caused it. I just didn't know what else to do. I didn't know what to say or how to help.

When COVID shutdowns started happening in April, there were no more outpatient programs, no support groups, no AA meetings. Everything was canceled. Everyone was on their own. Between his family and the sudden lack of resources, our marriage disintegrated rapidly. There were no emergency meetings for Neil in moments of weakness. There were no friends' houses for me to run to, to vent my frustrations over chick flicks and Chinese takeout. I was scared and heartbroken and guilt-ridden. How could I have not seen? How could I have not known how bad it really was? "Where was I?! Where the fuck was I?" I would scream to my therapist on the phone every week. "Where was I . . ." I felt ashamed, but I felt angry too. So, so angry. Why didn't he tell me? Why didn't he think he could tell me? Why didn't he ask for help? There was nowhere for me to go when I didn't know what to do with all of those things. The downstairs bathroom was all I had.

When a friend sent me a photo of a black-and-white speckled dog that had been found dumped on the highway in southern Utah, I didn't even run the idea by Neil before agreeing to foster her. I needed to feel like there was something I *could* save. It wouldn't have mattered anyway. That dog only spent two weeks with Neil.

Our trial separation started in early April. He stayed in Salt Lake City. I went south. I loaded Bucket, Dagwood, and the black-and-white dog into the van and drove three and a half hours out to one of our favorite expanses of desert. That first night, I watched that little dog following Bucket and Dagwood diligently across the horizon as the sun set. She sniffed what they sniffed, peed where they peed, glanced back and forth between all of us with her smitten, cartoon puppy dog eyes. She didn't seem to have the faintest idea that she had been brought into a war zone . . . that her morale boost was quite literally saving my life. She was the only reason I laughed those days. I couldn't lose her too. So I named her Birdie, and she became the first thing that had only ever been mine.

For weeks, I was parked out there with the dogs—the most uncertain, yet somehow the most content I'd felt in a long, long time. I was used to being alone out there. I didn't *feel* alone out there. In every other part of my life, Neil was like an extra appendage, always there, entrenched in every minute, every memory. His absence in all of those places was startling, crippling. Even after the second week of no contact, I still looked at my phone hourly just in case. But being alone out *here* felt natural. It felt downright normal. Between the pandemic and the state of my marriage, it felt like the only *normal* thing I had left. Those three straight weeks were the longest I'd ever spent in the desert. It was the closest I had ever felt to the dream we'd long had. To live out there, to build a home out there, to start looking the way Dagwood looked out there. Like he just . . . belonged. But as those weeks went on, I felt a tinge of guilt every now and again. I actually liked this version of me out there. And there hadn't been a version of myself I'd liked in a very long time.

At the end of the month, I arrived back at the house in Salt Lake

City. Neil and I sat across the table from one another. It was the longest we'd ever gone without speaking in over ten years. Making eye contact suddenly seemed uncomfortable. He wasn't even looking at me when he said he wanted to stay separated. He was looking down at his phone. He had pulled up the Verizon website so we could get to work on separating our phone plans. I sat, once again, staring straight down at my knees, my fingers tightening around the long, gut-wrenching letter I'd written him. I didn't want to stay separated. I wanted things to go back to normal. I wanted to go back to the desert and I wanted him to go with me. But I resorted to rage to hide my devastation. "You want me gone?" I shouted, standing up from the table, "Fine! I'm gone!"

Having lived in a van for so long, I had very few belongings that I actually cared about. Packing took no time at all. But even as I loaded Bucket, Dagwood, and Birdie up into Bertha, I had no intention of getting divorced. I figured we would stay separated for a little while, work on ourselves for a change. But deep down, I didn't think it would come to any of that.

In the beginning, I drove the dogs up to Salt Lake to see him every few weeks. I'd pull up in front of the house I used to live in. I'd send Bucket and Dagwood running down the driveway I used to park in. Then I'd speed away as quickly as possible, skidding to a stop around the corner, hyperventilating, sobbing into the phone to my mother with Birdie furiously licking at my face. Having her when the other two were with him was the only way I made it through those visits.

Neil never gave a time specification or a deadline. And I was too proud to ask him how long he'd like me to go away for. I was too afraid of what his answer might be. So the parameters of this separation seemed a mystery to us both. Other than the dogs, there was no reason for us to communicate. I was always the one to initiate the visits. If I didn't, they didn't happen. So, one day I stopped initiating. And he never asked. New information would come through in waves over the next few months. He quit his job. He was drinking again. He accidentally lit the backyard on fire. Our lifelong best friends saw no choice but to kick him out. He cut them all off, blamed them the way he blamed me. He moved away with the first woman he met on that dating app. The one with the photo of us. And he never saw Bucket and Dagwood again.

I understood that a clean slate is often the key to recovery for many addicts, but that last part hurt the most. That last part was impossible to explain. For months, Dagwood ran after every white pickup truck he saw rumbling past on dirt roads. I'd call out to him each time, watching his urgent trot slow to a standstill. He'd turn back to face me. *I'm sorry, buddy*, I'd cry. He did it for almost six months before he realized it wasn't ever going to be Neil behind the wheel. I couldn't decide which broke my heart more. When he started doing it, or when he finally stopped.

The clicking of Dagwood's nails coming toward me down the hallway brought me back to the waiting room. His left leg was shaved and stitched in an upside-down L-shape. He had a crooked, three-inch square shaved just above his left eye, as if they'd only tapped the buzzer to his fur to reveal a perfect red puncture. His left ear—also shaved—had white stitches along the top edge that made it look like he was wearing several tiny hoop earrings. But he was smiling. That dog was always smiling.

I leaned in, pressing my face into the thick, coarse fur of his neck, and whispered, *This is one of the worst haircuts you've ever had.*

chapter six

The Nosebleed

I have come to find that there is a societally acceptable amount of time one is allotted to grieve before it starts to make everyone uncomfortable. Eventually, people run out of things to say. They don't know how long they're going to have to comfort you. They don't know if they're even qualified anymore. Should they call someone? When will this be over? How long are you going to be like this? I knew people loved me, but many of them started to back away. I couldn't blame them, but I also couldn't trust them. I couldn't trust anyone anymore.

I became convinced that friends—both lifelong and recent—were in on the online harassment, the subreddit, the creation of dozens of fake accounts with names like briannamadiaisadumpsterfire and briannaboughtstolenland and briannamadiaisascammer. I tried desperately to report each account, but when one was deleted, they just made more. Instagram was no help, but Reddit actually shut down the initial subreddit. They notified all the participants that it was causing their target (me) suicidal ideation. Apparently, my mother had reported it enough to get the actual website's attention. But that didn't matter either. People not only laughed, but celebrated the idea that I might *actually* kill myself because of the things they were doing and saying. So they just went and started a new one. Then they contacted every company I had ever worked with on social media, saying whatever they needed to say to get them to drop me. *She's a liar! She's a fraud! She's a white supremacist! She is so problematic! She threatened me! She ran her dog over!* It was always "she" ran her dog over. "She" hit her dog. I was the only one who ever said "we." My attempts at protecting Neil from blame were so effective that it had apparently become my duty to shoulder all of it.

A handful of people would make dozens and dozens of anonymous accounts to send what amounted to hundreds of messages. "Damn trolls," one representative for an outdoor brand said to me over the phone. "I'm so sorry, Bri, if we post anything about you, they just fucking bombard us." I lost every single partnership I had, despite most of them outright acknowledging that they knew it was all nonsense. Albeit, there was one dog food company that responded to an angry tweet directed at them about me. They wrote that they were no longer working with me, which was news to me. I found out I had been "fired" via Twitter. Reddit was overjoyed.

Next, they began going after anyone who was associated with me at all. Friends, former co-workers. If I mentioned anyone, was in a photo with anyone, or, God forbid, anyone mentioned me, they were torn to shreds. The same fake accounts would descend, threatening to do to them what they were doing to me. I was too much of a burden for my friends to be around. I had very little income left. Total strangers had effectively blacklisted me from my own life. People online claimed to have known me from childhood, or college, or seen me just recently out in Moab. They claimed I stole merchandise from stores, that my dogs attacked them, that I had screamed some profane thing at them. Nothing was true, and so many people knew it. But no one did anything. No one said anything. I was hung out to dry . . . left to fend for myself, like I had been for as long as I could remember.

When I learned that Neil and his family had joined in the online harassment, it broke me entirely. I was alone in a room of the house belonging to my friend Gina, the very last friend I had in that town. I dialed my mom's number, and sobbed the whole situation into the phone with snot running down my face. She said she could barely make out the words I was saying. She sounded scared, but for the first time, she also sounded angry. When I had no words left to say, I waited for hers to come. "You need to stop, Brianna," she said, sternly.

"Stop what?"

"Stop ALL of this!" she screamed back, suddenly. I held my breath. "Stop looking at this shit! Are you trying to kill yourself?" She was yelling louder than I had been when she first answered the phone. And her voice only grew louder with each passing sentence. "These people aren't going to stop. And Neil? Neil isn't coming back, Brianna. The man you knew is sick, he's gone. He's *GONE*,

Brianna. And whoever he is—whatever he is now—you wouldn't want him back anyway."

My breathing switched to hyperventilating. She continued on, telling me the truth I was desperate not to hear. But my grieving time was up.

"FUCK YOU!!!" I screamed. It was the only thing I could muster. I hung up on her, threw the phone violently down onto the carpet. The dogs stayed perfectly still, curled up around me on every side, encompassing my body like a life raft. "FUCK!" I screamed again . . . but to nobody this time. My body crumpled forward. I could feel the veins surging in my neck. My eyes were nearly swollen shut from crying. I knew the pain was emotional, but I'd never felt anything so physical. I rocked back and forth, chanting aloud, *Help me. Help me.* It felt as though I was actually dying. Suddenly, a surge of warmth rushed over my hands and down my forearms. When I opened my eyes, everything was red.

Despite having had plenty of nosebleeds as a kid, and even having a blood vessel cauterized in high school, I was still floored by the amount of blood coming from my face. It was like someone had turned on a faucet. I bunched up the bottom of my T-shirt and held it to my nose. When I stood, the gravity change seemed to increase the flow tenfold. My shirt was soaked through in a matter of seconds, the blood trailing across the floor in huge, wet splats. I reached for a towel, quickly swapping it out with my shirt. The bottom was so saturated, it immediately started dripping down the front of my legs. I stumbled backward onto the couch and pressed the towel harder onto my face, but that only squeezed the blood out the sides onto my cheeks. Birdie licked at me frantically, her white snout dappled bright red.

Gina was in the front yard working on her mountain bike. I reached for my phone, knowing that I would surely pass out if I tried to stand up again. I dialed her number. When she didn't pick up, I sent a text, my finger smearing blood across the phone screen.

Help.

Only a few moments later, footsteps came thundering through the house. Gina ripped the door open and gasped. Blood coated the entire bottom half of my face, slicking my teeth, streaming down my neck onto my chest. My hands were clutching the towel I now held on my lap. It was so soaked, it had become too heavy for me to hold up. I couldn't stop the bleeding, and I couldn't stop crying, which made the bleeding worse. By the time Gina passed me off to the emergency room nurses, it looked like I had been in a car accident.

Due to COVID, masks were required by everyone in the hospital. I must have bled through three of them before they told me not to bother anymore. The doctor clamped my nose shut with a little blue, padded contraption, and once the bleeding slowed, he cauterized the blood vessels. My mouth tasted even more metallic than it had when it was filled with blood. A nurse I recognized as someone I'd seen out in town came in and held my bloodstained hand with her purple-plastic-gloved one. Normally I would have found that comforting, but all I could think was . . . *what if she tells someone*? I was on new medication that was helping with the mania, but it did nothing for my ever-increasing paranoia.

They sent me home with the blood-covered nose clamp and instructions to "try to stay calm." It felt rather humiliating. The hysterical woman in the waiting room who can't get her shit together. Gina informed my mother what had happened. She was terrified, but she still seemed so angry. She knew I was strong. I had always been strong. I had never been the one to fall apart. I couldn't be. Someone had to take care of her after my dad left. Someone had to take care of me. She didn't recognize this version of me, and it scared her. It scared everyone. But I had finally let myself let go. I finally let myself break wide open. "You should have just let me bleed out," I said to Gina as she tucked me under a blanket on her couch.

A week or so later, I dragged myself from bed in the middle of the night. My phone was buzzing incessantly on the floor next to the outlet I was using to charge it. *What the hell is going on*, I muttered to the dogs. I had two missed calls and a two-minute voicemail from Neil. I stared, stunned for a moment. We hadn't spoken in over a month. We were still just "separated," our lives still in limbo. He was dating already, clearly, so I wasn't sure what he was waiting for. But I was dating too. And I wasn't sure what I was waiting for anymore either. I had started to come to grips with how this all might end . . . that it probably *was* going to end. Regardless, I called him back immediately. He had flipped another truck. I urged him to let me come to the hospital. I told him it was okay, that he was going to be okay. He told me he loved me, that he missed me. But he turned cold suddenly, as if a switch had been flipped. He didn't want me to come to the hospital. "I'm fine. Don't come!" he shouted, in fact.

I didn't cry when I hung up the phone. I was too stunned. *He's gone.* My mother's words echoed in my head. *The man you knew is gone.* I climbed back into bed, wrapping my arms around Birdie's neck. It wasn't until the following morning that I remembered he had left a voicemail right before I had called him back. It was two minutes and seventeen seconds long. My finger hovered over the play button . . . but I never clicked it. To this day, I have never played that voicemail. I would be lying if I said it doesn't still haunt me sometimes. Those are technically the last words he ever said to me. But something deep, deep down told me I didn't want to hear them. I didn't need to hear them. My mother was right. Whatever this had become . . . I didn't want it anymore.

chapter seven

Two-Hundred-Dollar Bill

Long before my life went sideways, it went in a very different direction than anyone I had known as a kid in middle-class Connecticut. My best friend Mary was no exception. We met as grade-schoolers amidst the chaos of a YMCA swim class and, despite being as different as night and day, we had been friends ever since. Having once considered applying to law school herself, Mary decided it best to fly out to Moab to help me file for divorce. The mania that had helped me whip up years' worth of paperwork to buy my property had all but subsided by then. The idea of going through what I assumed would be an extensive legal process seemed impossible, but felt urgent. After Neil's accident, my mother called to tell more truths I didn't want to hear. Only this time, I knew I needed to. "If he hurts someone . . . God forbid, if he kills someone . . ." She paused, as if holding her breath. Since the nosebleed incident, she seemed to be more cautious about her delivery. "Legally, you're tied to him. If he messes up, they could come after you, they could take everything. They could take your property, Brianna." I cried for a long time after we hung up, but it was a different sort of cry. There was still so much sorrow, but some acceptance had started to creep in. I had to choose between my marriage and my land. So I chose the one that felt safer.

I picked Mary up from the Moab airport, which is *one* room where *one* fifty-person commuter jet shows up *once* a day. "Baggage claim" is a metal table outside the chain-link fence separating the parking lot from the tarmac. I watched as they pushed Mary's suitcases out. I knew they were hers, of course, because amidst the pile of sensible black roller bags, was a 1950s leather trunk with full belt straps and gold buckles, and an old Victorian carpet bag that looked like it had been taken off the set of *Mary Poppins*. It wasn't uncommon for her to travel with a typewriter. Frankly, I was surprised she didn't bring it to add some flair to the divorce papers she intended to type up. My smile spread from ear to ear.

I wouldn't call my divorce "messy." There was no back-and-forth over alimony payments or assets, no shouting over some lawyer's big mahogany conference table like you see in the movies. In fact, I had decided there would be no lawyer at all. I printed the papers off a government website. In one of the paragraphs, the default language read: *The marriage between Petitioner and Respondent is irretrievably broken.* Irretrievably broken. I was surprised to find language like that in such official paperwork. It felt oddly emotional, devastatingly poetic even, amidst paragraph after paragraph of legalese.

Mary was genuinely amazed that one could just print some papers off at the local copy shop and call it a divorce. Regardless, she insisted on typing up some clauses to add in about my book proceeds and dog visitations while I lay—practically incoherent—on the ground beside her. She was also adamant about finding a *real* lawyer in town who could go over the papers one last time before I filed.

A quick Google search revealed that there were three lawyers in town and only one whose website mentioned divorce. I looked on in a dazed sort of amusement as Mary put on a button-down shirt, a pair of tortoise-shell reading glasses, and a slick of bright red lipstick. "What is this, *Legally Blonde*?" I laughed, as she emerged from the bathroom. I was most likely a little drunk. It was almost 1:00 p.m., after all, and those days, I preferred everything to be a little blurry. My laughter became almost maniacal by the time we arrived at the law office. And by law office, I mean a side door in the driveway of the lawyer's house. And by lawyer, I mean the man standing in that driveway wearing cargo shorts, waving at us. Mary shifted the van into park and turned to look at me. "Brianna . . ." But I was already laughing again. "This is small-town shit, Mary; we're not in Connecticut."

"Well thank God for that, at least," she mumbled, sliding precariously off the driver's seat to the pavement nearly half her height below. We had always shared a mutual disdain for the place we'd grown up.

As we approached the lawyer, he pointed back at Bertha. "I've seen this thing around!" My heart raced. Once inside, Mary locked eyes on a framed two-hundred-dollar bill. Shifting her gaze to the lawyer's face, she spoke in a low, completely deadpan voice. "What is that? That's not real money . . ." He chuckled as he reached across the table to grab the papers she had organized into three separate paper-clipped piles. "Yeah, it is."

"No . . . it's not." I glanced back and forth at each of their faces as if watching a tennis match. He breezed over her retorts, appearing to try to hold back laughter himself. When he stood to grab something from his kitchen a few yards away, she spun to face me. "Brianna, that isn't even—"

"Mary, I love you, but please shut up . . ."

I imagined this lawyer logging on to the internet to share that the girl with the big orange van was a total fucking bitch by association. Years later, I would run into his wife in town, who assured me that he had not forgotten (and never would forget) that particular consultation. That did nothing to help my paranoia. "Your friend gave him such a hard time about the two-hundred-dollar bill," she laughed.

"Oh my God, please tell him I'm so sorry, she's a real spitfire, I hope he wasn't—"

She cut me off. "No, no. He thought it was hilarious!" I let out a huge sigh of relief.

"Well, good then," I laughed, "that makes two of us."

. . .

When I dropped Mary off at the airport, she kissed my cheeks, kissed Bucket, Dagwood, and Birdie, and handed me a stack of manila folders. She had organized everything by date and secured Post-it notes to the front of each. I sat in the driver's seat after she had gone, flipping through them one by one. *Bring this one to the courthouse in Salt Lake. Mail this one to Neil. Include expedited filing fee check in this one.* The fourth and final folder's Post-it read: *You're gonna be okay.*

chapter eight

840 Feet

Despite having half the property loan left to pay off, I took out another loan shortly after I filed for divorce. My land was beautiful, but it was also inaccessible by any means other than my two feet. I would drive the forty minutes out there from Gina's house every day and sit, parked out in the road, watching the dogs galivant around all sun-soaked and bright-eyed. *Look what Mama got for you!* I had shouted the first time I brought them up there after signing the title. Cupping Dagwood's face in my hands, I leaned in and whispered again. *Look what Mama got for you . . .*

The second loan was peanuts compared to the first, but it felt much riskier. I had started selling stickers and merchandise off my website to try to supplement the income I'd lost at the hands of total strangers. No one wanted to work with me on Instagram, so I had to get creative. I had to get us home. And when I bought the place, I never anticipated how much it would cost to bulldoze a driveway through some dirt. The loan company gave me a frighteningly short turnaround window to pay them back, but it didn't matter. I had to get us home.

Several weeks later, a gentleman in his early forties met me up there. He wore a baseball cap and a sweatshirt that read CANYON COUNTRY CONSTRUCTION. The dogs bounded in from all directions, and he immediately dropped to his knee to greet them. I smiled and breathed for what felt like the first time since I'd watched his white pickup truck round the corner toward us.

"Beautiful place!" he said, glancing up at me from amid the dogs' frantic licking.

"Thank you," I said, turning to admire it as if I didn't stare at it in bliss all day to begin with. He stood, shoving his hands into the pockets of his jeans, glancing from side to side as if we were expecting someone else. "Just you up here?" he asked.

"Yep," I said. "Just me and them." I pointed at Bucket, Dagwood, and Birdie, who were still milling about beneath his feet sniffing at his jeans, which I assumed probably smelled like his own dog. He raised his eyebrows in what seemed like an uncontrollable reaction. Like one's leg kicking out automatically when the doctor taps their knee with that little mallet.

"Really? Okay . . ." He looked puzzled. It wasn't the first time I'd gotten a reaction like that, and it certainly wouldn't be the last. Having driven a ten-foot-tall, bright orange van with thirty-five-inch tires for years, I was used to men raising their eyebrows at me. At a gas station just a few days prior, a man leaned against the front of his pickup truck at the pump across from mine. He was checking Bertha out, which was relatively uneventful. Bertha is impossible not to check out. As I rounded the corner to climb back into the driver's seat, he hollered over with a smirk, "Where'd you learn how to drive that big ol' thing?" I slammed the door shut and leaned out the open window. "Same place you learned to drive that little thing," I said, nodding toward his truck. I was giddy that I had come up with that retort in the moment and not after replaying it in my head in the shower later like usual.

"So, what're ya thinkin', then?" the driveway guy said as he stepped back to scan the property from east to west.

"Well there's a pretty significant wash that it's going to have to cross over, but other than that I just want to make sure we don't take out any living trees."

"Umm . . ." he chuckled, glancing at the junipers that surrounded us in every direction.

"I mapped a route," I offered hurriedly. He raised his eyebrows once again. "Okay let's see it."

I held my arms out straight on either side as wide as I could, imitating what I was intending to be a car. Really, I looked more like an airplane weaving up toward the top of the hill.

"We could move these two dead ones," I said, soaring along as he followed behind. "I think maybe we'd have to blast some rock right here and then . . . it might be a little bit of a loopty-doo around this tree," I called back to him. He had stopped to crouch down and examine the rock, but looked up at me, amused.

"A loopty-doo . . . okay. That's actually . . ." He put his hands on his hips and turned around to survey the path we'd walked. "That'll work." He nodded at me, satisfied. "That'll actually work perfectly." I rode that high for days.

The driveway ended up being 840 glorious feet of winding dirt, weaving around every single tree I had pointed to that first day. Three different culverts had to be put in to withstand possible flooding in the various washes that snaked down through the property. Some were much bigger than others, but water decimates the desert faster than you can imagine. Better safe than sorry. The top of the driveway ended in a miraculously occurring level dirt clearing surrounded by some of the tallest junipers on the entire property. I wanted to impact the perfection out there as little as possible, and thus far, I had been able to.

I was still technically crashing at Gina's place in town, but I started staying at the property as often as I could. The dogs could be free up there. I could be free up there. I had such anxiety about leaving those nine acres that my body reacted as though it was physically dangerous to do so. Sometimes I'd pitch a tent, but most of the time, I'd sleep in Bertha. She was still bare bones inside, just a mattress and a bench seat with a few wooden drawers Neil had built. But there was something wrong with the transmission, and I didn't have Neil around anymore to fix her or even diagnose her. So with each passing day, I held my breath as she lurched more and more violently up the steep switchbacks to the top of the mesa. I could see the reddish droplets seeping from beneath her like blood. It was a problem I was openly choosing to ignore, but was rapidly becoming something I'd have to face. I had sold the only other car I had ever owned. The idea of a *third* loan was terrifying. But not as terrifying as the notion of not having a way to get back up there whenever I wanted, which was every single day. I refused to give Bertha up. I just couldn't keep playing whack-a-mole with the quirky problems of a van as old as I was. Reluctantly, I financed another used Jeep Wrangler from a dealership up in Salt Lake City. I'd had pretty good luck with those, after all. Not to mention, a Jeep is just about the most sensible car one can have in a wild open desert like Moab.

As for Bertha, she became a part of the décor up there. A big orange blob whose mere presence was still a tremendous comfort to me. Always will be. I talked aloud to her as often as I talked to the dogs. *Good morning, Bertha*, I'd say, all sing-songy. I leaned against her back tire one afternoon in the first bit of morning sun, smoking a joint while the dogs were out exploring their paradise. *We'll get you fixed up someday, girlie*, I said between puffs. *Promise.*

Financially, I was in absolutely no position to build a house. Most days, I was too terrified to even *look* at my bank account. My Instagram work was still stalled out entirely, except for a few affiliate links and merchandise sales. The advance money I'd received to write my first book amounted to everything I had in my savings account. And that had gone toward the very ground I now stood on. Not that it wasn't worth it, of course. I had bought myself a home . . . there just wasn't a house at my home.

I came up with the idea to start looking at trailers one afternoon as I drove through Gina's neighborhood. Almost every other house had some old, dilapidated white RV or tow-behind that looked like it had been melting there in the sun since they closed the uranium mines in the eighties. *I bet people sell those things for real cheap*, I murmured to Birdie, who was always the one in the front seat. My mother was adamant that I not go buy "another old, broken fucking thing." "Don't talk about Bertha like that!" I snapped back into the phone.

"Just go to a dealership somewhere, somewhere with a warranty. Please, Brianna, for God's sake."

The following weekend, Gina's now-fiancé drove me up to Salt Lake City in his baby blue pickup truck that made those terrible popping sounds from the exhaust every time he accelerated. But who was I to talk. I knew all about what it meant to love an old car. In the half-back-seat, Bucket, Dagwood, and Birdie paced back and forth, fogging up the windows. On my lap rested a shoebox with my two ball pythons, Bean and Mae, inside. I had found someone up in Salt Lake City who offered to watch them until I could get my living situation sorted out. Gina was more than happy to see them go.

When I arrived at the dealership, I was overwhelmed by row after row of brand-new, tacky trailers with red racing stripes on the sides or names branded on the back like *The Vortex* or *Elite Adventurer*. After the much expected, raised-eyebrow, *what's-a-girl-like-you-doing-here-alone* routine, the salesman informed me that he was a proud owner of a 2019 Vortex himself. "I don't need something that . . ." I hesitated. "Fancy." He shrugged and we continued down the lot toward the used trailers. There was a thirty-foot 2010 trailer in pretty decent shape.

It was still awfully shiny for my taste, but it didn't have some bizarre name emblazoned on the back of it, so that was a start. It smelled sterile inside, like a hospital. It came with all the furniture of course, given that everything was nailed into place.

"A new couch has been put in," he said, motioning to a crisp, black leather love seat adjacent to a small dining table with fixed benches on either side.

"My dogs are gonna destroy that couch," I mumbled.

"How many dogs ya got?" he asked, motioning for me to peek into the bedroom alongside him.

"Three," I said, scanning the brown bedding with matching brown curtains.

"Oh, they'll love it," he exclaimed. "My dog can hardly contain himself whenever he sees us loading up the Vortex for the weekend." Making small talk with just about anyone used to be my specialty. Now, I was willing to write a down payment check on a trailer just to get out of what felt like a social situation. Even normal human exchanges felt exhausting. They felt like culture shock from the desert bubble I had begun to create for myself.

When I left, I called my mom to tell her. She seemed pleased with my decision, but I felt nothing but regret. I couldn't see myself on that leather couch, in that overly brown bedroom. Nothing about that trailer felt like home. Nothing about that trailer felt like *me*. I was tired of living in other people's spaces. They all felt foreign and unreliable. I had been living out of a few suitcases for more than six months by then. I felt like I couldn't exhale. I was always holding my breath, waiting for the moment I'd have to pack them up again. Other people's homes reminded me every single day that I had lost the only person who had ever felt like mine. I felt stuck in those places. Stuck mourning my past in the midst of everyone else's present. Stuck watching Gina and her now-fiancé plan their wedding while I checked their mailbox each day to see if my finalized divorce papers had arrived.

I checked into a motel room shortly after leaving the RV dealership. I was exhausted and COVID was still enough of a concern to keep friends from opening their doors to folks just passing through. One friend did text me just moments after I collapsed onto the scratchy quilt. It was the link to a Facebook Marketplace listing for a 1986 travel trailer that a young couple had remodeled just for fun. The outside was painted matte white with orange, yellow, and brown retro stripes. It looked like something out of the seventies. There were two doors on one side. One in the front and one in the back, which were a whopping fifteen feet apart, given that the entire trailer was only twenty-two feet long to begin with. Inside, they had put down laminate wood-grained flooring and hung floral wallpaper behind the futon in what one could call "the living room." The entire left-hand wall of the trailer was what you could call "the kitchen." A row of cabinets painted green. Beneath them, a sink, two feet of counter space, and the tiniest little oven I'd ever seen. The stovetop had some rust, but they'd put in a little white tile backsplash. The bathroom had a cream-colored fringe shower curtain and a potted plant next to the palm-size sink. "The bedroom" (aka the mattress in the back corner of the trailer) was surrounded by windows and framed by an accent wall of shiplap wood they had painted a speckled, vintage white. Above the foldable "dining table" hung another potted plant and a little painting of a woman with a flower in her hair. *There it is*, I whispered to Bucket, who had fallen asleep with her head resting on my thigh.

It took much less convincing than I was expecting to get the RV dealership to refund my deposit. The old "damsel in distress" trope seemed to come in handy in that regard. I bought the 1986 trailer for less than half of what I would have paid for the other. When we came to pick it up, it was sitting in the grass in the front yard, surrounded by wandering chickens. It looked like a little fairytale. Gina's fiancé hooked it up to his trailer hitch, and we took off back to Moab. The goal was to make it there before dark, given that none of us could figure out how to connect the electrical from the truck to the trailer's rear lights. It took only six or seven attempts to successfully back the trailer uphill 840 feet of winding dirt. Only one juniper tree was injured in the process, though thankfully, it wasn't life-threatening.

The trailer looked significantly smaller the moment the dogs burst inside, snouts to the ground, sniffing every inch of new space. They pushed past each other in the tiny hallway, resorting to walking backward when they realized it was too crowded to turn around. There was almost an equal amount of dog-to-floor space. There was also no power whatsoever. I dragged a few bags from the back of the Jeep into the trailer, using my phone flashlight to guide me. It was still early spring, so nights got cold fast. I fumbled around in the dark for the sleeping bags I had brought in from the Jeep, then swung by Bertha to grab more pillows and blankets from that bed. I almost choked up while doing so. *You're not being replaced, Bertha, I promise.* I patted her sliding door as if she were a giant dog.

Once I'd buried all four of us beneath all the blankets, I propped my pillow up beside the windows surrounding the bed, leaned my head back, and looked up. I had seen the stars up there so many times already, but never from bed. Never from a nest of blankets in a den with my dogs. I don't know how long I sat there looking up. I only knew I wasn't anymore when I woke early the next morning, still propped ever-so-slightly against the window. I usually dreamt about Neil. I usually had nightmares about *something*. But not that night. That night I just . . . slept.

I stood up to let the dogs out. *Can you believe this, guys?! We're STANDING UP! We have our own front door!* They pressed all of their noses up to it, as if to see if they could push it open themselves. As I watched them dart off into the brush, I realized we'd spent enough time up here already for them to each have a designated direction they liked to run off in first thing in the morning. We were making routines. For the first time in a long time, something had started to become the same.

I stepped out into the morning light and snapped a photo of the trailer on my phone. It occurred to me only then that I hadn't yet told my mother about the last-minute trailer swap. I loaded the dogs up into the Jeep and drove down the road to the one corner that gave one bar of cell signal. The fact that there was no service up there had quickly become one of my favorite things about it.

My mom picked up on the first ring. "How'd it all go?" she asked excitedly.

"Okay, don't be mad," I said, "she's only four years older than Bertha."

chapter nine

The Deck

My first order of business was to build a deck. Not only would it double my technical "living space," but it would also hide the unsightly, dried out rubber wheels the trailer sat on top of. It also seemed like a reasonable first project, given that a deck was basically just a wooden rectangle, right?

"Wrong," the man at the hardware store said. I had done some of my own internet research on what I would need, but those lists were based on the assumption that whoever was trying to build an entire deck likely had at least a basic set of tools. Besides the screwdriver that had been rolling around in one of Bertha's drawers for the last four years, I had not one tool to my name.

"So, I'll probably need . . ." I looked around at the shelves surrounding me. "A hammer, obviously. I'm gonna need a hammer." The man raised his eyebrows, amused at how clueless I was. By the time I hit the register, I had spent close to five hundred dollars on tools and I still had *maybe* one-third of the tools I was told I would need.

That afternoon at the gas station, I ran into a construction worker I had slept with the summer before. Just the usual nightmares of small-town life. But he was a beautiful young thing, so I forced small talk for a few minutes. The moment I mentioned the deck, I wished I hadn't. He wanted to help. He was in construction, after all. I hesitated.

"Bri," he chuckled, "c'mon, I have a truck *full* of tools." I perked right up. "All right, fine. Tomorrow morning? I'll drop you a pin to the property just don't . . . don't tell anyone where I live, okay?" I said, flatly.

He stared back, extremely perplexed. "Okay?" Unbeknownst to me at the time, people on the internet had already used public records to find my address and satellite images of the property to share on the subreddit. Anyone who wanted to find me had been provided everything they'd need.

Over the next few days, he showed me how to use all kinds of different tools. A handsaw, then a table saw, then a grinder. Sitting behind me on one of the long wooden planks, he wrapped his arms around me, his hands pressed on top of mine, showing me the proper pressure to apply to the sander. It was sort of like that scene with Demi Moore and Patrick Swayze in *Ghost*, but there were a lot more splinters and I couldn't wait for him to get off me.

The deck we built was beautiful. So beautiful that I wanted to take credit for the whole thing, and became furious with myself when I knew I couldn't. Still, I was incredibly grateful and incredibly adamant about paying him for his work. He gladly accepted. In my mind, that meant I never had to see him again. Something he only found out when I immediately stopped answering his calls.

Despite not having built it entirely on my own, I still thought that deck was one of the most beautiful things I'd ever seen. It was about eighteen feet long and eight feet wide with two big posts on either corner. *Needs a little somethin', though, don't ya think?* I asked Bucket, who had already begun to pant in the midmorning sun. It was late spring, much to my relief, so the nights were warming up. But the days were too. *We're gonna need some shade around here, huh?*

I walked over to Bertha, who had become a sort of "garage" for the time being. The tools I had managed to acquire were piled on the front passenger seat. I grabbed the cordless drill and some screw-in hooks and climbed up on top of the trailer. The metal creaked, denting under my weight, as if it might give in any second. I screwed the hooks directly into the metal. Birdie shot up from the dirt, startled by the high-pitched grinding. I hadn't quite considered that drilling holes in one's roof might not be conducive for certain weather events until they were already drilled. There were plenty of times I still found myself "coming to" in the aftermath of a questionable decision.

Back down on the deck, I stood on a slowly ripping camp chair to screw two more hooks into each corner post. Using some thin black paracord Neil had left in the back of Bertha, I tied a big white sunshade to all four points. *Voila!* I exclaimed, as Bucket reclined beneath this newly fashioned umbrella. Dagwood came over to inspect my work, sniffing at the shadow on the wood. I grabbed a rug from the back of Bertha and sat back in my camp chair, admiring our oasis, looking around for something else to do. I had a chaise lounge with a bright orange cushion I had placed in the dirt out in front of the deck for maximum sun exposure. *We could fix up The Yard*, I said, scratching my chin. *A walkway, maybe?*

The excavator that dug out the driveway had blasted through several feet of rock in one spot. The machine had pushed the remnants off to the side, forming piles of thick, surprisingly flat stones ranging from one to three feet wide. I stood staring at one particularly perfect stone with my hands on my hips. Birdie had assumed I was staring at something that had crawled *underneath* the rock, so she was now furiously digging at the dirt beside it. I didn't stop her. I needed all the help I could get. *No way in hell we're gonna lift this, y'all*, I said aloud to the dogs, all three of whom had gathered around by then. After a few moments, Bucket got bored, wandered back up the driveway, and plopped herself back down on the rug I had laid out. That's when I got the idea. *Watch out, Buck*, I said as I jogged up to the deck and yanked at the rug. She leapt up, visibly annoyed.

I carried it under one arm down the driveway, a shovel under the other. I dug a decent amount of dirt out from beneath the front side of the rock—with the help of Birdie, of course—until it started to tilt forward ever so slightly. Positioning the rug beneath it, I ran around the other side of the rock, got on my knees, and pushed. I knew I'd have better luck pushing than pulling. The rock slowly flipped forward and down onto the rug. The underside was caked with still-damp dirt from the last storm. A lizard darted out frantically, immediately followed by Birdie and Dagwood in a cloud of kicked-up sand. I pushed the rock forward in one more slow rotation to get it semi-centered on the rug. Grabbing the top corner of the rug, I started dragging it up the driveway toward the trailer. Birdie was immediately enthralled with this game, grabbing onto the other end of the rug as if we were playing tug-of-war with a one-hundred-pound rock. I laughed aloud, watching her back legs dragging along up the driveway, tail wagging.

Once I'd reached the dirt patch between the deck and the lounge chair, I flipped the rock over twice more, end over end, until it rolled off the rug and hit the ground in a puff of dust. *Would you look at that?!* I exclaimed to Birdie, whose teeth were still firmly clamped on the other side of the rug. Elated, I rolled the rug up once again and headed off down the driveway.

This went on for hours. In my flipping and dragging technique, many of the rocks broke, which was always upsetting after spending such a long time picking out the best ones. But eventually, there were seven large stepping stones all in a line. I walked east a little ways toward a grove of dead junipers and gathered up the smoothest, most interestingly twisted limbs. Junipers are one of the few things I've always found more beautiful in death than in life. I lined the branches up alongside the stones to accentuate the path. *Just to add a little flair*, I said, winking at Bucket, who was, once again, back on the rug. With the sun setting, I poured myself a glass of wine, put on some music, and strutted down those rocks like it was Fashion Week in

Paris. Birdie and I lay on the lounge chair together, watching the last of the light disappear. *We're gonna need to find some heavier branches tomorrow*, I whispered to her, as we watched Dagwood dragging one up onto the deck to gnaw on.

For days I hopscotched up and down that walkway, swept dust off each stone religiously (even though sweeping anything in the desert is futile). Sure, I had simply moved heavy rocks from one place to another, but I had *figured out* how to move them myself. I started looking around for more things to do. I had learned almost immediately that being aimless is harder than it sounds. Even harder when your only companions don't speak, and you're still learning to survive your own thoughts. I wanted projects. Things with my hands, things with long, detailed instructions telling me exactly how to succeed, exactly how to put something back together, exactly what the end result was supposed to be. I needed something methodical, unemotional. There was a comfort in that, perhaps, because there was no instruction manual for whatever the hell else I was doing with my life.

chapter ten

The Half-Wolves

On the wall of my grandmother's condo hung two taxidermied deer heads. I used to sit beneath them, staring intently into their glazed, plastic eyeballs, willing them to come back to life. This new décor was startling to the rest of the family, as my grandmother is one of the most die-hard animal lovers one could ever know. She once sent all six of her grandchildren an email briefing about a very concerning situation taking place in her garage. She couldn't catch a small field mouse that had found its way in, but she didn't want the cats to catch it either. A conundrum, for sure. All this to say, dead deer nailed to the wall were out of character. She explained that she had found them at a roadside tag sale and couldn't bear to leave them there because she didn't want them to be lonely. And somehow, believing that these severed heads were sentient, emotional beings in need made far more sense than any other answer she could have given. It was as though the whole family exhaled and said, *Oh yes, of course.*

My grandmother's real name was Nancy, but she was Nanny to us. I remember running through her house as a child, followed closely by the eyes of silky black cats on the spiral staircase, or perched atop the piano. There were always at least four or five of them that only she could tell apart. I hung on her every word as she regaled me with stories of her childhood best friend: a white farmhouse duck named Huey. The two of us would walk down the beach together, hand in hand, stopping to gently right any horseshoe crabs who had found themselves upside down, unable to make it back out with the tide. Their alien-like bodies looked so helpless, legs frantically kicking out into nothingness. I'd call out to them as they slid back through the sand into the water. *Goodbye! Be careful next time!*

Nanny and my grandfather divorced after having been together for more than fifty years. They even had a big fiftieth wedding anniversary bash just before they called it quits. That story usually makes people rather sad, but for some reason, I still smirk when I think about it. Perhaps because my grandmother had decided that, after all those years, she just wasn't happy anymore . . . but she believed—in her late seventies—that she still had time to be. That she still deserved to be. And I think there is something beautifully optimistic about that.

After the divorce, she moved to that condominium, decorated it with abandoned deer heads, and started setting traps out by the dumpsters to catch stray cats and re-home them. Many would end up staying with her, of course, acquiring outlandish names like "Chicken" and "Edna-Tuggy." One of her favorite cats—a big orange tabby named Cordelia—died back in the late nineties, but Nanny would still talk out loud to her. Well, not to her, but to her ghost, who she was convinced was living on top of the refrigerator because the cereal boxes were always falling over. Whenever we went out to dinner, she would ask the waiter for a box to collect every last scrap of food on each of our plates. These always went straight to her cats, and by her cats, I mean the ones in her kitchen and the ones out by the dumpster. The neighbors were never pleased.

I knew she qualified as the "crazy cat lady" type, societally mocked by men and women alike, but even as a kid, I envied the way she lived. After my own divorce, I understood it completely. To surround oneself with the unconditional love of animals, to be able to save something in a world that often seems unsavable? That made all the sense in the world.

I suppose it is not hard to see where my feverish love of animals originated from. It's also not hard to see why I named my first dog "Bucket" or decided, on a whim one afternoon, to foster eight seven-week-old puppies in a twenty-two-foot trailer with no running water in the middle of the desert.

I had been living up on the mesa for over a month. We had entered the second year of the COVID-19 global pandemic. The world was still unrecognizable, people were still terrified, the vaccine was still in development, and some of the busiest, most crowded places on earth were still silent. And I watched it all happening from that little trailer out in the desert. I was used to silence.

The little local shelter in town is called Underdog Rescue Moab. They work almost exclusively with the Diné people in the Four Corners area of the Navajo Reservation. The reservation, which spans across Utah, Arizona, New Mexico, and Colorado, is roughly the size of the state of West Virginia. And yet within that territory, there are fewer than *four* veterinarians. A simple spay or neuter procedure can often require a three-hour drive across a desolate expanse of desert. Factor in the cost of gas, and it becomes unfeasible for so many, no matter how much they love their dogs. So Underdog holds four or five clinics in various parts of the reservation each year. Volunteer veterinarians come down with huge, RV-size trailers built out with full medical facilities inside. They offer five-dollar rabies shots and affordable (often free) medications for things like fleas, ticks, and worms. They also perform anywhere from thirty-five to fifty spay and neuter operations per day. The majority of the dogs actually surrendered to Underdog are puppies. Entire litters of them since most of the dogs that folks were bringing to be fixed had *already* given birth.

When COVID hit, it hit Indigenous communities harder than most any other population in the United States. So it was no surprise that a whopping *ninety-two* dogs had been surrendered at a clinic in just one day. Now, surrendering any dog to a shelter is often chastised, judged, chalked up as a form of cruelty. I myself am guilty of once thinking this way. But had three different families not all consecutively decided that Dagwood was too much for them, too wild, too *this*, too *that* . . . he'd have never ended up where he belonged, which was, most certainly, with me. To understand and admit that you cannot care for an animal or provide the type of life they need is *honest*. To seek a solution to better suit that animal? That isn't *cruel* at all. If the stigma was removed, perhaps we'd have more dogs safely brought to shelters as opposed to neglected or chained up or dumped on the side of the highway.

Underdog had posted on Instagram, detailing the overwhelming number of dogs they had taken on. *Desperately in need of fosters*, they wrote. Later that evening, as I sat on my porch, looking around at my entirely-off-grid, twenty-two-foot, sans-running-water trailer . . . I wondered just how *desperate* they were.

Many rescues—albeit, with best intentions—have foster requirements akin to college applications. You must have a nine-foot-tall fence and approximately thirty references and home visits are required and that home cannot be an apartment or a condominium, and it sure as shit can't be a trailer parked out in the middle of nowhere. In order to adopt Bucket all those years ago, I wrote down a fake address and crossed all fingers and toes that they wouldn't request a home visit. If they had, they'd have discovered the truth—that I was actually living on a thirty-foot sailboat with (once again) no running water, air conditioning, or basic amenities of any kind. I cannot stress enough that I understand these rules are set with best intentions . . . but no dog I've ever known would choose a five-by-ten-foot concrete and wire cell over a cozy little apartment or a daily walk around a condominium complex or the spray of sea mist from the bow of a boat.

I called Underdog to see if—despite my living arrangement—they would let me foster. I had barely finished the sentence before the volunteer said hurriedly, "Can you take a litter of eight?" Almost instinctively, I felt the need to ask permission from someone, or negotiate with a roommate, or *beg* my mother like I had for every animal I ever saw as a child. But this was *my* property. This was *my* life now. I didn't need to ask anyone to do anything. *Eleven dogs in a twenty-two-foot trailer?* I thought to myself. *Yeah . . . why not.*

The first time I held them, I could fit four of them in my arms at the same time. They couldn't have weighed more than three pounds each. At first glance, they looked like they couldn't have possibly come from the same mother, but "rez dogs," as they're called, are the ultimate mutts. *You never know what you're gonna get*, Forrest Gump would say. Two of them had fluffy, black fur with white markings on their faces. One had a brindled coat that was as short as a pit's. Two were white, but only one of those was fluffy. One was brown with distinctive little eyebrows, another brown-and-white-spotted. One had a marking on his forehead that looked like a rising flame.

I drove slowly up my driveway, easing through every turn, as though the two travel crates full of puppies were actually full of glass. Bucket, Dagwood, and Birdie rushed out the trailer door and straight to the Jeep, as if they had smelled them a mile away. They surged around the crates as I lowered them both to the ground. Birdie's tail wagged eagerly. Dagwood's ears stood perched toward the puppies' high-pitched yaps. It only took half of a puppy to emerge from the first crate for Bucket to turn on her heel and leave, as if she'd just stepped into the wrong meeting room. She was as interested in them as I had assumed she'd be. Dagwood was most certainly amused at first, but had no problem playing the disciplinarian role. Some folks on Instagram were outraged by the videos I would share of Dagwood baring his teeth or lowly growling under his breath when the puppies would clumsily roll across his back as he slept or pull his ear just a bit too hard while they played. Those types of gestures from dogs can be intimidating if you don't speak dog. And a lot of people don't speak dog. By then, dog was pretty much *all* I spoke. I could have written subtitles for each of their interactions, used a laser pointer on a giant photo of Dagwood's body language like a college professor. Not only did it fascinate me, it just made sense to me. It was straightforward and concise, and most importantly, it was honest. *Stop. I don't like this anymore. Pay attention to me. I love you.* So many situations don't call for much more than that, but humans are brilliant at complicating everything. I've always preferred the company of dogs.

Some of the puppies were slower to leave the crates that first day, and I had no intention of rushing them. Curiosity gets the best of every puppy, so I knew it wouldn't be long. After only a few minutes, I was shuffling my feet up toward the trailer, thirty-two little paws the size of half-dollars scrambling all around me. Unbeknownst to me at the moment, this is how I would be walking 80 percent of the time for the next two weeks.

Once inside the trailer, they scattered (as much as one *can* "scatter" in a trailer that size). I knew I'd have no problem keeping an eye on all of them when we were inside, and if the way they had followed me up the driveway was any indication, I'd have no problem keeping an eye on them outside either. That night, I spread pee pads from wall to wall in front of the couch and lined all the corners with old blankets and beach towels I'd bought from the thrift store. I took the lid of a heavy-duty plastic storage bin and wedged it upright between the stove and the bathroom door; the space between those two places was as wide as the Rubbermaid itself. *Ta da!* I sang, stretching my arms out dramatically. The storage lid effectively sliced the trailer in half. Each side even had its own entrance. *Your side*, I said to the puppies, before spinning on my heel to face Bucket, Dagwood, and Birdie, who were perched up on the bed. *Your side.* They slept in bed with me every night anyway, but I wanted to make a quiet space for my three when they needed a break from tiptoeing over a pile of spilled puppies just to get to the water bowl. Now their water bowl was right at the base of the bed. (The memory is vivid because I stepped directly into it two nights in a row when getting up to pee at 3:00 a.m.)

I'm going to start calling this your "wing," Dagwood, I whispered, as he nuzzled his head up underneath my chin. *And that's the puppy wing. Or maybe the nursery, whattya think?* He sighed and stretched his legs out long in front of him.

One two three four five six seven eight.

I must have recited that aloud twenty-five times a day. Initially out of due diligence, but eventually just out of a sing-songy habit.

After all, a litter of eight seven-week-old puppies isn't hard to find. Instinctively, they seemed to know not to wander off. They'd follow me around like ducklings, tumbling their clumsy, loose-limbed bodies over rocks and roots to keep up. They would pause momentarily to sniff at the sagebrush or tap their little pink toes at a passing bug before looking up and frantically scurrying back to the pack. When I'd stop to sit in the shade of a juniper tree, they would pile up onto my lap, or press themselves against my legs, snuggling into the crooks of my knees, resting their heads atop each other's sleeping backs. It would have been physically impossible for them to get any closer. One. Two. Three. Four. Five. Six. Seven. Eight.

The sound of their little claws barely scratching the surface of the trailer floor was what woke me up each morning. Though it was more of a whisper than a sound. I'd lay perfectly still, holding my breath, listening to them toddle about, relishing in the first (and last) lazy moments of my day. Then the whines would start, then the yips, and finally the full-blown barks. That was my cue.

There was always going to be one inevitable pile of puppy poop, but anything less than five was a great night. They had plenty of space to pick a spot that they wouldn't end up stepping in, but the blankets were a lost cause. I never wanted them to be without cozy blankets at night, so I kept two clean sets. On the third day, I'd drag both urine-soaked sets down to the laundromat in big black garbage bags. It was messy, and smelly, and exhausting, but I was always smiling and cooing and comforting. Few roles had ever come so naturally to me, had ever made the chaos of it all fade into the background. I can't imagine motherhood is all that different. I'm sure that's why some feel so called to it.

In the mornings, I would feed my three first. Only when they had finished did I feed the puppies, because feeding puppies is like a game of Hungry Hungry Hippos. After breakfast, I would make my coffee on the stovetop while they piled up just inside the open screen door, peering out at the world from what surely must have felt like a den. It certainly felt like a den to me. When my coffee was ready, I'd announce, *Children! Let's stroll the grounds.* Off we'd go down the driveway, eight clumsy puppies tripping over each other, trying to keep up with the older three. Birdie would pause every now and again, leaping around to face them, to egg them on, make them believe they were going to catch her. But just as they approached, she'd be gone again. *Too slow!* I'd laugh, as she tore back off into the brush. I was usually bringing up the rear, strolling calmly so as not to spill the coffee from my Freddie Mercury mug, which simply read, THE SHOW MUST GO ON. And that's sort of what it all felt like. Like some show. Like my favorite movie from childhood, *Fly Away Home*, about the girl who finds a nest of abandoned goose eggs and raises them, teaches them to fly just like their mother would. Those two weeks in the desert, roaming around with eleven dogs, were some of the happiest times of my life . . . plopped amid some of the darkest.

Two weeks later, all but one of the puppies left for their new homes. All but the little fluffy black one with the perfect white nose. "It was just the way he looked at me." That's the only answer I've ever been able to come up with as to why within just a few hours of bringing those puppies home, I knew I'd be keeping that one. "He looked at me as though we'd met before." And there's really no other way to describe it. That very first night, I squatted down over the pile of them. He was the only one that wasn't asleep. He blinked up at me as though he'd just hatched from an egg. I smiled at him, which sent his tiny tail into a frenzy. *Banjo*, I whispered, planting a kiss on the center of his tiny forehead.

There really wasn't a reason in the world why I couldn't have a fourth dog, after all. My days were spent running around in the desert with three as it was. And four is really not much more than three. It still only occurs to me that having that many dogs isn't all that common when I see the look on other people's faces in response to "These are my dogs."

"All of them?!" they say, wide-eyed. Though, to be honest, I had the same reaction once to a woman who said "These are my kids," while gesturing to the small sea of blond heads bobbing around below her. She had so many children that some of her children had to help hold the other children. But be it dogs or kids, there is a certain point at which some people decide you've gone overboard. If I had consulted with anyone about the decision to adopt a fourth dog, perhaps they'd have said something along those lines. Perhaps they'd have said it was a bad idea. But since I hadn't asked anyone, it was a great idea.

As Banjo got older, it became apparent that he was completely oblivious to how small he was. As a puppy, his tiny bear paws nearly dwarfed his legs, which led me to believe that he would grow up to be quite big as an adult. In fact, I was certain he would be the largest of them all. Larger than Bucket, who was sixty pounds. But Banjo would only end up being thirty-five. The smallest one of the pack by a decent amount. His coat stayed fluffy, but faded from black to a brindled brown. I remember realizing one afternoon that his fur now looked exactly like the chocolate and peanut butter swirl ice cream that was melting down my hand and onto the deck. I laughed aloud as a drop landed squarely on his back. He was bewildered, but thrilled when the other three began to lick him feverishly.

He was truly the youngest kid: bolstered by the examples set by his older siblings, but fiercely protected by them too. It was Bucket, Dagwood, and Birdie who made him feel like he was bigger than he was. He was born into a pack and never left it. It was clear he'd never been backed into a corner, never been outnumbered, never been left to fend for himself. So he grew into a tough little shit who snuggled sweetly into the shape of his siblings at the end of each day. Exhausted from all the shenanigans that are only tolerated from the baby of the family.

He would catch a scent on the wind and charge off through the sagebrush, disappearing between a grove of juniper trees, emerging moments later on the heels of an entire pack of wild horses. They would trot ahead of him, seemingly entertained at his audacity, before stopping abruptly to face him. *We've played along, now piss off*, I imagined them saying. Banjo would trot himself back over to me, beaming.

Bucket and Banjo didn't really interact much. They lived alongside each other just fine, of course: drinking from the water bowl at the same time, snuggling up against each other beside me in the trailer when the 3:00 a.m. chill set in. But the relationship between them was about as distant as their ages. Bucket was ten years old when Banjo showed up. A decade divided them. Bucket had lived a whole lifetime with me before that pudgy puppy came into our world. A life that twinkled in the haziness of her aging eyes. A life that wore itself across the white fur of her face.

Their only real meaningful interaction was hunting. It seemed that Bucket relied on Banjo for his quickness of sight, for his willingness to check each patch of sagebrush. He would leap off toward any little thing that moved, any little leaf that rustled. Bucket would watch stoically, knowing not to waste her energy unless the odds were in her favor. Knowing things only old dogs know. Banjo's body language—especially that tail, that feathery, glorious tail—would signal that it was not, in fact, a leaf, but one of those sneaky lizards they were always after. Bucket would charge over and join in the investigation. Banjo would wait expectantly as Bucket surveyed the brush, pressing her snout to the sand and blowing up little puffs of it past her whiskers. If she began to dig, the chase was on. Banjo would dive in beside her in enthusiastic lunges, tossing dirt up behind him with both front legs at the same time. Banjo's strong, young limbs and Bucket's trained nose.

Birdie and Dagwood would often go over to investigate, but lose interest quickly. Birdie was the type to look at one thing for approximately eleven seconds before seeing a butterfly and chasing that off into the distance instead. Dagwood was uninterested in prey of such size. Over the course of his ten years of life, he had killed three rabbits, one beaver, one muskrat, two voles, countless rats, and *lost* a battle with two porcupines. He had once attempted to drag a domesticated goat up the side of a cliff by one horn. The goat was completely fine, albeit lacking in any survival instincts whatsoever. I'm positive the porcupines were fine too, because how any animal ever actually *defeats* a porcupine is beyond me. Not to mention, I'd have noticed even the smallest trace of blood or fur during the hours I'd spent with a pair of pliers pressed to his snout, plucking out quill after quill. And while he *had* killed his fair share of animals, each and every one was considered vermin. Any old hunter or kid with a BB gun could have shot 'em and skinned 'em into a hat without the blink of an eye from most folks.

I never *enjoyed* the death of any animal, of course. I've been vege-tarian since I was a teenager. I cried each and every time, placing little flowers or rocks beside them. It seemed a sort of apology to them, as well as an offering to the vultures who would inevitably arrive soon to finish the cycle. But how could I be upset with Dagwood? He was an animal doing things animals do. You don't get mad at a coyote for chasing a rabbit. In my eyes, Dagwood was no different. He was a Carolina dog. A breed of dog that was only domesticated as recently as the 1970s after they were found roaming in the swamps of North and South Carolina. Their mitochondrial DNA places them at the very base of the biological tree from which all dogs throughout his-tory have stemmed. In many ways, for many reasons, he was far more than a dog.

There were some folks who said my admission of Dagwood's wildness on social media might encourage other people to let their dogs become murderous little misfits, to which I usually rolled my eyes. *As though the average neighborhood poodle even has the instinct or physical ability to hunt something down in the first place.* If they had ever witnessed the speed and agility with which those jackrabbits moved across the desert with Dagwood on their heels, they would know he was more than dog too. They'd see there was something wild about the both of them.

I never tried to hide that my dogs and I lived this way, and I caught a lot of flak online because of it. *Ugh. City people,* I'd mutter aloud to Dagwood after reading outraged comments about some perfectly normal dog thing my dog did. These city people (I'm allowed to call them that, by the way, because I used to be one. I threw a fit about visiting Montana as a teenager because I thought it was "a wasteland." I grew up in Connecticut, okay. Our family chihuahua had shoes). These city people spoke so confidently to me from behind their phones about things they knew nothing about. It's bizarre to feel the need to defend your use of Utah's public land to a dental assistant who lives in a condo in Delaware with her Jack Russell terrier, and has never even *been* to Utah.

It's hard for some people to grasp what it's like to live somewhere far away, somewhere different than everything you've ever known. I didn't grow up knowing that there were millions of fields and forests and cliffs and mountains and canyons with all different kinds of land designations and recreation rules. I didn't know that Utah alone had 22.8 *million* acres of public land. That's roughly 42 percent of the entire state. I didn't know you could just turn down any old dirt road out there and drive until the whole world disappeared. I thought the "Wild West" was something that only existed in movies. I didn't always know what it's like to unclip the leash from a dog's neck and watch them dart out across wide-open desert. Of course that would seem *wrong* or *illegal* somehow if all you'd ever known was Private Property signs and leash laws. It's hard for some folks to imagine that kind of freedom still exists out beyond their fenced-in yards.

Once upon a time, those concepts were mystifying to me and my shoe-wearing chihuahua too. I understood why folks were so curious. I just never understood why some of them were so damn angry. I hadn't once advertised my Instagram as some sort of dog training page or "how to" account. I never wanted it to be. I just was who I was, and I did what I wanted to, and I shared most of it, but certainly never all of it. But that's the exact concept social media had slowly begun to kill. To be unique and different and exciting is rewarded. But only if it's in the ways that people are comfortable with. Only if it's in the ways that don't make them question what they thought they knew.

I suppose some of my beliefs about dogs can seem at odds with each other. I have an extensive collection of Halloween costumes I'd bought for them over the years. Dagwood had a chiropractor after his accident; Bucket has a neurologist to this day. I have entire drawers full of joint supplements and probiotic powders and single-ingredient salmon skin flakes to sprinkle atop their entrees like a Michelin-starred restaurant. Not to mention, the cost of feeding four dogs top-shelf food is like a rent payment each month.

But Banjo has also been drinking from whatever muddy puddle of water he could find since the day I brought him home, something he most certainly picked up from the other three. None of them ever got sick. Their systems just adapted, I suppose. They learned to avoid the prickly pear cactus that dotted most every desert field because I let them walk right into 'em. They only needed to do that once or twice before they realized they should probably keep an eye out for those. Eventually, their paws became so calloused from the hot rocks and dry earth that they wouldn't feel it even if they had stepped on one.

They were always getting little cuts in their flesh from stray barbed wire or fallen branches, playing rough with each other, or wandering off on their own personal adventures. It never crossed my mind that they might just "never come back." *If he don't come back, he ain't your dog*, a friend's grandpa once told her. (I like to imagine he doled out this wisdom from a wooden rocking chair on a rickety farmhouse porch somewhere, but have never wanted to fact-check in case that isn't true.) I love my dogs like humans, but I think to *truly* love a dog is to treat them like one.

Of course I inherently understood the risks of a life lived like this, for both myself and my dogs. "Bad things could happen out there!" people would say. People who had yet to learn that bad things can happen anywhere. They saw wild animals as villains lurking in the shadows, waiting to pounce on the first human being in sight. "What if a pack of coyotes eats your dogs?!" a woman once said. As if the average coyote isn't the same size as the smallest member of my pack. As if a pack of coyotes surrounded by hundreds of square miles of their natural food sources would risk trying to overpower four large dogs. The coyotes out there are fat and happy.

"What if the dogs come across a snake?" I knew my dogs had to have come across *plenty* of snakes in all the years of free roaming they'd done, so I just figured there was something instinctual that told them to keep away. Something that was still left over in some dogs even after we started messing with their genetics for our viewing pleasure.

I once came across a perfect rattlesnake shed that had gotten caught on a single cactus needle. It swayed gently like a wind sock. Bucket leaned in cautiously on the very tip of her front paws, but recoiled backward before she even got within six inches. Watching Bucket fleeing from a paper-thin layer of skin that was once part of a snake confirmed what I'd suspected. Hell, that instinct is still left over in many humans. Petroglyphs and pictographs carved into caves and canyons depict snakes beside fires, tongues outstretched, coiled up as though perfectly poised to strangle the life from something. Even modern-day religions use snakes as representations of sin or evil, if you buy into that sort of thing.

One afternoon in 2017, Neil and I were lying in the sand beside our raft when a Great Basin gopher snake swam across the river and right up onto the beach.

"That's a rattlesnake, Bri," Neil screamed, leaping up from the sand on which he sat. I leapt up too and walked toward it.

"No, no . . . See, look!" I said as I approached the snake from the side, slowly bending down to grab hold of its body. "You always want to take hold of it near the bottom third of its body. You think of snakes in thirds, I learned that from Steve Irwin!" I said, as I walked back toward Neil with the snake in my outstretched arms.

"You're fucking crazy right now," he shouted, scrambling backward.

"It's not a rattlesnake, it's just a gopher snake. Common mistake! Their coloring is so similar, and the gopher snakes have even evolved to flatten their heads out and try to mimic the shaking of a rattlesnake tail! Isn't that so cool?!" I shouted, as he stared at me dumbfounded. In that instance, Bucket and Dagwood ran for the hills as well, so the whole snake thing really didn't cross my mind much after that.

People's fear of the natural world was startling. They believed that certain places needed "conquering." That the weather had a vendetta somehow, and wild animals were just monsters waiting behind every corner. Everything was out to get them. But nothing could be further from the truth. Perhaps what truly frightens people about nature is how little they actually matter to the whole operation out there. How it spins on without them no matter what. The fear of being meaningless is more frightening than death.

In 2018, I read an essay by author Emily Ruskovich called "The Half-Wolves." It recounts the story of her childhood dog and the remote Idaho ranch they grew up on. She tells of an idyllic family who spent years out in the woods on long walks with their spirited bluetick hound, Annie. It was harsh, rugged country. Not once in all their years had they seen another soul out there until the afternoon that Annie was killed. It was just Emily's mother up there with her, walking an old logging road that cut through the side of the mountain.

Suddenly, a lone, weak, but wild-eyed woman appeared from around a tree, surrounded by her five feral half-dog half-wolves. She couldn't get them under control fast enough. Annie never stood a chance.

I was heartsick for Emily's mother, enraged on her behalf. She was just a woman out strolling through the woods with a loyal dog at her side. Emily goes on to write, "For a long time, I was filled with rage at that woman and her five half-wolves. Who has five half-wolves?" *Exactly!* I thought to myself, the first time I read it. They buried Annie in the pasture, and for years, I seemed to remember that being the end of the story. Annie in an unmarked grave . . . Emily's mother . . . they were all I could remember, because I saw myself in them. I could see myself having been right there in the woods beside them.

That essay popped into my head one afternoon as I sat panting, covered in dirt, up against the stump of a pinion pine on the backside of my property near The Caves. Bucket and Dagwood had managed to outsmart a rabbit, cornering it into one of the deep nooks in the rock. I'm sure the rabbit thought there was a way out on the other side . . . but there wasn't. Bucket's bark was piercing, echoing off the walls of the stone half-circle the rabbit was pressed up against. Dagwood snapped wildly in the very few inches of space that separated his teeth from one of its hind legs. Banjo was the only one small enough to fit all the way in, since the rabbit was just as big as he was. Regardless, he joined in the barking and lunging as if it were half his size. Birdie peeled around the corner, hearing the commotion, and started digging alongside Dagwood, making the opening deeper with each frantic stroke. I know this kind of thing happens all the time. I know that rabbit doesn't know the difference between a pack of dogs and a pack of coyotes. Being hunted each and every day is just how life works out here. But I felt compelled to stop it this time. One, because I might actually be able to, and two, because it just didn't seem like a fair fight. That rabbit didn't stand a chance.

I dove in alongside them, scooping Banjo up, attempting to contain him under one arm like a football. He wriggled violently, still barking and lunging toward the hole. With my other hand, I grabbed Dagwood's collar and dragged him backward, his bark turning raspy as he strained against it with all his might. His eyes were fixated. He'd gone primitive. Nothing but that rabbit existed. With no free hands left, I tried shooing Birdie away with my foot, but just then, the rabbit attempted to make a run for it. Bucket sprinted to the other side, knocking me to the ground in the process. *No, Bucket! No! No!* The rabbit fled back under the rock, unscathed, but surrounded once again. Banjo had gotten loose and was back to adding to the chaos with frantic, high-pitched yelps. I knew he didn't yet have it in him to inflict any real damage, so I used my free hand to grab hold of Bucket's collar instead. *Stop! Birdie, stop! STOP! NO!* By now, my naked stomach was flat to the ground, clutching Bucket and Dagwood by the neck, as they dragged me forward like sled dogs. I spun my leg around, attempting to put Birdie in some sort of choke hold with my knee. The dust was everywhere. I could feel it on my tongue as I screamed, *Go! Go, go, go!* hoping the rabbit might understand me, might seize the chance. Mere seconds before Bucket twisted herself from my grip, it dashed out, leaping straight over my sprawled-out legs. But those few seconds were all it needed.

All four dogs took off after it, kicking up even more dust. As I rolled over coughing, trying to blink it out of my eyes, I caught one final glimpse of the rabbit's back legs as it sprinted up over the top of the wall. It moved so fast, it seemed as though its feet never even touched the ground. The dogs would never catch it now.

I crawled into the closest patch of shade I could find, exhausted from the pandemonium. One of my knees was bloodied, and the sweat pouring from my forehead was turning the dirt in the corners of my eyes to mud. From my left hand sprouted a tiny cluster of thin cactus needles. I had plucked the last one from my palm by the time the dogs showed back up. Birdie arrived first, of course, because I had begun to cry. It was one of those pesky moments of clarity. This was chaos. I was out in the desert, alone, hiding out with a pack of unruly animals. And that's when I remembered how that essay really ended.

The woman with the five half-wolves was devastated, inconsolable about what they had done. She was from Switzerland. She wanted so badly to go back. She lived alone with those dogs in a trailer one might never even know was hidden out there in the woods. They were all born to her mother dog, and she had intended to get rid of them. "She knew it was crazy, she later told my mom. She knew it was irresponsible," Emily writes, "but her loneliness was such that she couldn't part with even one."

It was no longer Emily's mother whom I saw myself in. All I could think of now was what had happened to that woman. What had hurt her so deeply that she fled to the woods. She must have felt safe out there, surrounded by all those primitive dogs. So comforted by them piling around her at night to sleep. Perhaps out there, she could protect them, hide them away, hold on to their wildness because that was the magic of it all. She could try to do for them what no one could do for her. She could try to keep them safe.

"I think of her often," Emily wrote at the end of that essay. "Who knew that somewhere nearby, amidst all the chaos and hostility of those beautiful woods, was this kind and timid woman, living in some remote trailer, with only her half-wolves to love?"

chapter eleven

Routine

As time went on, my routine at home became simple . . . well, simple to me, I suppose. Living in the trailer was more akin to living in a model home, or a display room at your local IKEA. It was freshly painted inside, decorated with frilly pillows and cowboy hats I'd hung from the wall behind the couch. I spread seashells and animal bones and potted succulents along the windowsills. There was a sink and a shower and a toilet and a smattering of electrical outlets and light switches, but the trailer itself wasn't plugged in to anything. There was no power source, no town water lines to hook up. It was just . . . a metal rectangular structure that provided protection from most of the elements. In short, it was no more useful than the broken-down van it sat adjacent to.

My mother was astounded at my ability to make things harder

on myself . . . because that's how she saw it. That's how most people saw it. To a lot of folks, it probably sounds like a nightmare, having to figure out all the things that have become mindless. People get up and turn on the lights, they summon hot water from the faucet in a matter of moments, they adjust the thermostat with a flick of their wrist. They are the gods of their own little worlds, whereas I was mostly at the mercy of mine. But that was okay with me. The things I loved so much about my years spent living in Bertha all came flooding back. The ability to breathe through discomfort, to become malleable to the constant shifting of the earth, the gratitude for the simplest things. How often does the average person get out of bed and feel so thankful that they can stand up straight? Having one little closet to hang my coats felt luxurious. A drawer just for silverware? How lucky was I?

By the time spring drifted into summer, I was accustomed to being covered in sweat before 9:00 a.m. I'd sweep the floor of the trailer every now and again, but there was hardly a point. The doors and windows were open all the time, and sixteen paws tracking dirt in and out all day every day didn't exactly help. There was dirt and dog hair and sweat and drool and sunscreen and bug spray on everything. But living in what some might consider a sort of "squalor" made me feel tougher, more capable, more durable.

"You sound like you're describing a tire," Mary said to me on the phone one afternoon. She was beyond proud that I'd finally made my own home for myself, she just didn't understand why I picked one without a working toilet. The toilet *could* have been usable, but there was a big crack in the holding tank below that I didn't see when

I bought it because I just handed over my cash and drove away with the thing. So, without a toilet, I was diligent about timing my trips to town around my second cup of coffee to ensure I'd be able to make it to a restroom. If I couldn't make it all the way to town, there was a bare-bones rest stop a bit farther past my road in the opposite direction from town, and if I *really* couldn't make it, there was always the big hole I'd dug behind a boulder a couple dozen yards from the trailer. When I had to pee, I just peed on the ground. The dogs would all tumble out the door in the morning, walk out onto the dirt and squat, and I'd squat right beside them—eye level—like some feral child they had raised themselves.

Toilet aside, my trips to town were always strategically planned, which makes it sound like I was in an old Western movie and had to travel there by horse, but I digress. It's still quite an endeavor to make an hour and a half round trip to the nearest grocery store. So I'd consolidate my tasks accordingly. First, I'd pack up the Jeep with the usual: three five-gallon blue plastic jugs for water, which I called "blueys." A heap of garbage bags that I'd shove onto the front seat. Always the front seat. I'd once made the mistake of tossing the bags in the back where Birdie's claws ripped one of them open, spilling spoiled produce and coffee grounds all over the Jeep. Now, the only thing that went back there with them was my overflowing canvas bag of laundry. That, and a shower caddy holding my shampoo and conditioner and a faintly mildew-scented towel.

My first stop was always the Shell station at the edge of town for gas and water. In between the three pumps was a nondescript red spigot sticking up from the ground. I'd carry my blueys over, lift the spigot handle, and hold on to the ever-heavying jug as tightly as I could. That water gushed out with shocking force, but it was fresh, and it was free. Funneled from the underground water supply that snaked deep beneath the streets of town. If I was coming back from an excursion *north* of town, I'd turn down River Road and pull over to the natural spring. It flowed out of the red rock so pure that you could drink it straight. No filtering or boiling needed. I'd haul them back to the Jeep—one forty-two-pound jug in each hand—waving off the offers for assistance from men there to fill up their own. Just those ten gallons of water were good enough to last me and the dogs nearly three days.

After filling my water from either the Shell or the spring, I'd drive over and toss my garbage bags into the dumpster behind the dollar store. There were no overt signs that said Private Use Only like many of the other dumpsters in town had, and no one had yelled at me yet, so I just kept doing it.

I rarely had dirty dishes because I rarely ate, but every other week or so, I'd stop by the car wash with a bucket full of plasticware, plop it down on the ground in the middle of the stall, and aim the sprayer straight into the bucket. Folks in the neighboring stalls would turn to look as the occasional plastic cup bounced across the cement behind them, propelled by the power wash setting. On the way home, the bucket of dishes would sit on the front seat where the garbage bag had been. With the windows down, I could count on most of them to be dry by the time we got home, albeit covered in the same amount of dust as they were when I brought them down there in the first place. The fact of the matter was, there wasn't a chance in hell anything up there would ever *actually* be considered clean.

If the weather wasn't conducive for showering with my solar shower (a thick, black bag filled with two gallons of water, tossed on the deck outside to warm in the sun), I'd stop off at the Moab Recreation and Aquatic Center. It's basically a small YMCA-type facility, but there's a special price for locals: just five bucks for a shower. There were six shower stalls to choose from in the women's locker room, but the last one on the right-hand side had the best water pressure. In the colder months, I'd stand beneath the stream until it turned tepid . . . which wasn't very long at all. But when you don't have hot running water—or any running water, for that matter—it feels like a lifetime. I'd scrub my skin nearly raw, watching the water turn brown as it swirled in circles around the drain. Remnants of mud and clay from the Colorado River.

What little electricity I did have came from a small solar panel that I would position on the deck, and slowly rotate to follow the trajectory of the sun throughout the day. My computer and my phone were really the only things that needed charging. There was no cell service up there anyway. Most of my power went to strategically running my giant box fan. On a cloudless day, I could get a solid eight hours out of it before needing to charge up the solar again. This meant that I could charge it all day, untouched, to use for eight hours that night, *or* charge it and use it during the triple-digit daytime temperature, leaving no juice for the evening. I was a lizard when it came to the sun, and I desperately valued my sleep, so I went with the former. Plus, there was almost always the faintest hint of a breeze to survive on up on the mesa. Yes, of course I could have run everything off a generator, but I wouldn't have dared. The idea of staining the silence up there with the congested, gasoline-scented sputter of an engine felt positively sacrilegious.

The strongest Wi-Fi in town was at the library. The tables were almost always filled with bearded transients or dirt-covered rock climbers, or local raft guides who couldn't afford Wi-Fi at the apartments they were all jammed into. Most of the housing had turned to Airbnbs, displacing the very folks who made the town run . . . who served and guided and catered to the tourists who flocked in from all over. I'd tuck into a corner of the library—careful to avoid any sun-soaked chairs the notorious library cat had claimed—and check my email or download some movies on my phone. Every Wednesday, I connected to the library Wi-Fi from my car. I had to park as close as possible to have enough service to sob into my phone on my weekly teletherapy call while the dogs slept in the back. Oftentimes, I'd go wade into the river afterward, slip my head beneath the surface, and scream at the top of my lungs.

If I had laundry that needed doing, I'd pick up some takeout, toss a load into the jumbo washer at the laundromat, and watch one of the movies I'd downloaded with the library Wi-Fi. The Wi-Fi was pretty decent at the laundromat too, but not enough for streaming. The sink in the bathroom was nice and big, so it was common that dirtbags would go in there and wash their hair. So common, in fact, that management had to put up a printed sign on the mirror explicitly forbidding any more sink showers, and instead, offering a list of places throughout town where one could pay for a shower. That's how I discovered the locals discount at the Aquatic Center.

The trailer's fridge and stovetop ran on two forty-gallon propane tanks that only needed filling every three weeks or so. Since the fridge was more often on the fritz than not, I just gave up on it entirely. I'd grab a block of ice from the gas station instead. Always a block, never a bag. A bag would be a gallon of water by afternoon, but a block would linger in my Yeti cooler on the porch for at least a day and a half. As the ice slowly melted, I'd drain it out into the dogs' bowl for a refreshing midday drink. *Cocktails!* I'd yell out, hearing their paws crunching over snakeweed as they headed toward the trailer. I almost always heard them before I saw them.

As for me, the majority of what I drank was hot. Water, wine. Hell, even the coffee intended to be hot somehow got hotter if left unattended on the porch. I remember reading something about Chinese monks who believed drinking hot tea when it was hot out actually cools the body down. Whether that was true or not, I hardly cared. It all goes down the same pipe. And warm wine is basically just sake anyway.

I made my trips into town as quick as possible. I found myself rushing so frantically sometimes that I felt out of breath. Get in and get out. Don't let anyone see you. Don't let anyone know where you came from, where you're returning to. By then I had effectively cut out everyone I'd met in that town. After all, they had "met" some manic-depressive shadow of the person I *actually* knew myself to be.

Gina was only interested in me because she was "a fixer." But how can someone possibly "fix you" if they never even knew you to begin with? She had no frame of reference of what my baseline was. She had no idea where I was trying to get back to. Besides Heidi—who I'd cut out months earlier—no one in that town ever actually knew me at all. They knew me as "the girl with the orange van" or "the Instagram influencer" or "the girl who hit her dog" or "that drunk girl I saw sleeping in an umbrella."

My friendships (and lack thereof) were whispered about. Some romantic rendezvous or weird thing I did at a bar became fodder for online gossip. People claimed to *know* things about me, about my life. Even if they knew nothing, the internet still provided them the perfect place to pretend they did. The most reasonable thing for me to do was to sever every tie, disappear from all social events, hide up on the mesa and look down at the smoldering ashes of all the bridges I'd burned while I, myself, had been on fire.

As soon as my chores in town were done, I'd drive as fast as possible back to the mesa, back to the simplicity, to the place where I could actually breathe. There was no cell phone service there, no way for any messages to reach me. It was like sliding back into warm water after being tensed up and freezing cold.

Each night, as the sun set, I'd take my lighter from candle to candle, all along the countertop and the mantel beneath the glass windows. I lived entirely by candlelight and one small, battery-powered lantern that I would carry outside like an old witch, wrapped in a tattered shawl, calling out to the dogs through the darkness. I'd hear the clinking of their collars as they strolled back up the driveway from their summer night wanderings. As I held the screen door open for them, they'd file in—one, two, three, four—and the nightly rearranging routine would begin. *Banjo, Dags needs that spot so he can stretch out his leg. Birdie, leave Bucket alone please, we're not playing right now. Okay, Birdie, now your butt is directly in my face.* It didn't matter if it was 110 degrees, that dog absolutely had to sleep damn near on top of me. Eventually, we'd all settle onto the bed, and Bucket would let out her long, telltale *hhmmpphhh*, indicating that she had found the perfect spot. Then the silence would creep in. I wish I could bottle up that silence. Despite the temperature still being in the eighties at night, it made everything outside seem frozen in place. I'd blink in the blackness, waiting for my eyes to adjust. The light from the stars shone through the windows just bright enough for me to watch the dogs' chests rising and falling. I'd smile when, for a brief moment, all four were in sync.

chapter twelve

Wall Street

As much as trips to the dumpster and movies at the laundromat were a part of my routine, so became finding a way to survive the heat each day. By early June, temperatures had soared to the mid-nineties. There was air conditioning in the Jeep, so if we were running around somewhere on a particularly hot day, I'd drive home slowly with the AC blasting to bring all our core temperatures down a whopping two degrees before we stepped back out into the heat again.

From noon to about 4:00 p.m., the trailer was basically inaccessible. No amount of windows could cool that thing down with the desert sun beating down on it relentlessly, uninterrupted for hours on end. I'd run inside briefly to grab warm water or a melted tube of Chapstick, then retreat back to the deck beneath the sunshade. Shade does wonders in the dry heat.

The dogs would go down to what I called "the basement," which was really just the cool dirt underneath the trailer. A breeze would blow between the tires, and the sun never hit it. Some days, even I crawled under there. Eventually, there was nothing left to do but find water that we could sit in up to our necks.

The previous summer—our first in Moab—the Colorado River had been at record lows. So low, in fact, that multiple southwestern states started what became known as "The Colorado River Drought Contingency Plan," which included cutbacks to water usage in residential areas. There were four-hundred-foot-wide sandbars in the center of a river that once carved out the Grand Canyon. Due to their enviable obliviousness, the dogs were delighted by these new beaches, so we made the most of them. Gina and I would pack up a backpack full of wine and sunscreen and a little portable speaker and we'd wade out there to our own private island where we could both forget about the state of the world for a moment . . . where I could try to forget all the calls I'd been making to the suicide hotline . . . all the cruel messages lurking in my laptop. Seeing the dogs bounding through the mud, rolling in the sand, swimming after each other, racing out to grab the tennis ball . . . that made life seem worth living. So I tried to go out there as often as I could. Whether or not I cared about my own life anymore, it seemed only fair that the dogs get to enjoy theirs.

My spirits were a bit higher that following summer, but so was the water. I'd found a handful of beach spots that the dogs and I would alternate through, including that old sandbar that had shrunk in size, but was still visible. It was strange the first day I went back there on my own. Strange without Gina or Heidi or the husband I'd had for over a decade . . . the one I still thought of almost every day.

I sat on the sandbar with my legs in the water, watching Dagwood patrol the shoreline for beavers. Birdie was trying to snatch a stick from Bucket. She underestimated her older sister sometimes. Bucket was still sharp as a tack and whip-fast. Birdie wasn't gettin' that stick unless Bucket gave it to her. Banjo toddled his still-puppy paws alongside one curved corner of the sandbar, slapping at the skater bugs that slid across the glassy water. Those dogs made everything beautiful. Any pile of sand, any roadside meadow, any forest service road and muddy stream. They were the view I was after. The look on their faces, the way their bodies moved so effortlessly, the way the instincts still vibrated off their haunches. They looked how dogs used to before human beings insisted on "refining" them. They wanted them fluffier or smaller. They wanted longer ears or flatter faces. They wanted their tails chopped off for some reason. Although, who am I to talk about dogs with no tails? Granted, Dagwood's lack of tail was due to spinal nerve damage, not aesthetic. It was a gorgeous tail. One of the best I've ever seen. I squinted my eyes sometimes to pretend it was still there . . . pretend none of this ever happened.

My entire life revolved around those dogs. We were feral and unrefined and all the other things the world had told us not to be. I slept when they slept, ate when they ate, even went outside to go to the bathroom when they did. There weren't more than a few minutes each day that we were apart. We were a pack. So, when they got out of bed, I did too.

. . .

On one particularly hot day, I decided we'd head to one of our regular spots, the one with the deepest water. There was a road that went down either side of the river. Potash Road on river right, and Kane Creek Road on river left. Potash was much more traveled as it was a much longer, paved, relatively straight road that led up toward Canyonlands. There were also several road-trip-worthy stops along that side, including the famous Corona Arch hike and a popular stretch of sandstone cliffs known as Wall Street. Rock climbers from all over the world would pull up and belay each other right from the top of their cars from one of more than one hundred different routes. It was a dream crag.

Kane Creek on the opposite side had a few riverfront pay-to-park campgrounds and some private property. Just a mile down alongside the river, the road turns to dirt and cuts up left between the canyons. I based the quality of all our local jaunts on how likely it was to see another person out there. By then, I'd found dozens of incredible secret spots. I suppose that's the thing about the desert and all its cracks and corners, its ever-shifting shapes and rough edges like ceramic that hasn't yet been in the kiln.

While this particular river spot was perfectly pleasant, the walk out to it was less than. From a pullout on the side of the road, you skid down a shale-covered hill with several rubber tires at the bottom. On the left, an old pipeline stretches down toward a drainage ditch, where it sits half-submerged in green sludge water. This is a bit of an Indiana Jones moment, but we'd traversed it enough that we knew the drill. Bucket pranced across the top of the pipeline, her wet pawprints leaving a single straight line. Birdie would take a few running steps out onto the first half of the pipe and then use the momentum to leap over the second. The girl had major hops.

Banjo would walk face-first into the slime as if it weren't even there, so I always just waddled across behind him in case his little legs got stuck. Dagwood waddled behind me, utilizing the wake of slime-free water created by my shuffling feet. His bad leg made it harder for him to wade through heavy things like snow or mud, and he couldn't balance on something as narrow as the pipe. He had tried the first time we discovered this spot, lost his footing, and crashed down into the water. He was unhurt, just startled. I was too. I hugged him until he got physically annoyed, wriggling away like a preteen boy at school drop-off. He wanted to go play. He had long forgotten why I was even hugging him in the first place.

After the pipeline crossing, you follow its jagged, rusted remnants that jut out from the left side of the trail. But if you turned your head and looked out toward the river, the view was just fine. Plus, the whole tetanus-ridden pipeline thing was the reason this trail was so rarely traveled. There were plenty of beautiful places to go along the river, but very few where the dogs could run wild. That was the only kind of place I was interested in. My happiness was dependent entirely on theirs.

Access to "the beach" (aka an outcropping of large, smooth rocks) was a steep dirt slide that was best to take sitting down. By the time we'd actually make it there, all of our legs would be covered in green slime and my butt would be covered in dirt. But few things compare to slipping into a cool river after a hot sandy hike. I threw off my bathing suit top and waded in. Bucket followed me out immediately, having been an avid swimmer her whole life. Her white snout bobbed across the water with ease.

Birdie was relatively spastic in most of her movements, but none more than swimming. She would run and take a flying leap, lifting all fours off the sand and crashing down into the water. I constantly had scratches on my legs and stomach from her overshooting the landing and crashing into me with her outstretched claws. What she lacked in grace, she made up for with enthusiasm. Banjo ran back and forth trying to bite Birdie's legs, as if telling her to *calm down, for Christ's sake.* Dagwood took off to patrol the shore for beavers like he always did. I dunked my head under the cool, chocolate-milk-colored water before climbing up onto a flat rock to dry in the sun. For a while, I just repeated the pattern. Dunk. Dry. Dunk. Dry. I shuffled through some music on my phone, standing to dance and shimmy around every now and again. I called the dogs in for a stroll down the rocks together. All five of us crouched down to inspect the milky corpse of a crawdad. *Banjo, don't eat that, please. Banjo!* He stormed off toward the water for a dip. Dagwood cut up into the bushes toward the trail, and the girls and I went back to lying in the sun.

Only a few minutes had gone by before I sat up to do what I called "a dog scan." Much like with the foster litter, I'd look around and mumble, *One, two . . . three . . . where the hell is—oh there he is. Four.* Birdie and Bucket were still sunning themselves and Banjo was down on the sand. But when I turned to look downriver, all I could see was Dagwood's head. He was in the water, looking right at me just one hundred feet down, but he wasn't moving. The water was clear up to his chin, so I wasn't sure why he'd be standing there of all places. I called out to him, but he wouldn't come any closer. As I leapt a few rocks closer toward him, I realized he was swimming. He was swimming in place, fighting against the current. The water he was in looked positively tranquil. These were no rushing rapids or jagged rocks. He had found himself in one particular spot where the river whipped around a smooth sandstone cliff into a little inlet. The water was deeper in there and it was moving *just* a bit faster than the water around it. *Just* fast enough that he could keep up with it, but couldn't get ahead of it.

I wasn't worried. He was only about thirty feet away from the rock I stood on. But that was the very last rock. From there, the rocks turned to full-blown cliffs with no way to climb out. I'd have to swim down to him and we'd swim back up together. This seemed like no problem since I considered myself an excellent swimmer. I was the captain of my high school team, after all. I'd even held a state record for a few months. I jumped in, slicking my hair back, and paddled down toward him. I could hear the huff-huff-huffing of breath from his nostrils. When I reached him, I wrapped one arm around him and took some of his weight as I straightened my body and felt around for the ground with my feet. The water, it turned out, was far deeper than I thought. I couldn't touch. I had nothing to push us off from, nothing to gain momentum.

Now, the two of us were there, swimming side by side. If there was a bank to swim to, I knew Dagwood would have swum to it already. There was also no way for me to swim over and use one arm to traverse the rock wall while holding Dagwood's full weight under the other. I had developed a pretty impressive six-pack by then but I wasn't Rambo. Swimming against the current obviously wasn't getting us anywhere, so to continue to do so would be foolish. The only option was to swim to the other side of the river. The other side was the opposite of cliffed-out. It was a paved road. We could climb out no problem if we swam the three hundred feet across. *Well, Dags... look what we've got ourselves into this time,* I muttered, spraying him with water droplets as I spoke through heavy breaths.

I rolled over onto my back and positioned Dagwood across my stomach with his legs over either side of me and I back-paddled. With my head flat back, sun in my eyes, and my ears beneath the water, it looked and sounded more chaotic than it actually was. When I took a break to lift my head, Dagwood looked like he was resting on a pool raft, eyes half-closed as if he were falling asleep. *Are you having a nice time, Dagwood?* I rolled my eyes and continued paddling.

Somewhere around the middle, I went to right myself to take a break, when I felt my feet hit sand. *Aha!* I shouted, standing straight up. The water was only mid-thigh deep, but still too deep for Dagwood to stand, so I knelt over slightly and held on to him like a football bobbing in the water. When I stood, Bucket barked from the rocks I'd left from. *No!* I screamed. *Stay!* Birdie and Banjo sat stoically. If they came after me, we'd all just have to float to the other side together. What a scene that would be.

The plan was to swim across, climb out, run back up the road a decent way *past* where we had been sitting on the other side, climb back into the river, and swim across, this time, with the current working in our favor. The plan was solid, but the development of this new patch of sand made me wonder if we'd have to do that at all. *Maybe we can walk back up from here, bud.* In just ten feet, the water dropped off immediately, the ground untouchable again in every direction. *Okay*, I laughed. *Plan A.*

Perhaps that sounds absurd . . . that I'd laughed. But I'd survived enough terrible things at that point that I felt confident in my ability to discern what was actually worth freaking out about. I'd held Dagwood for six hours as he lay broken and bleeding to death. I'd lived on the floor of a veterinary hospital for a month. I'd changed his diapers, the ones the doctors thought he would have to wear for the rest of his life. I sat holding my breath through six different surgeries, waiting for someone to come out and tell me whether or not he had lived through it. Once you've done all that, standing in the middle of a cool river on a hot day with said dog was *not* something to panic about. Worst case scenario, I would just hang out there in thigh-deep water until some poor, unsuspecting river guide floated by. And knowing my luck, it would probably end up being the one I had slept with.

I could still see Birdie's little white speckled coat against the red rock by the time we finally made it to the other side of the river. I was completely winded, but Dagwood stood up as soon as he could touch the bottom, shook off, and immediately resumed patrolling for beavers. I stood with my hands on my hips, surveying our next Indiana Jones–esque obstacle: a hedge of thickets ten feet wide and woven so tightly together it looked like their branches were tied in knots. *Fuck's sake, Dagwood!* I said, as if he himself had planted them here.

By the time we made it through, my bare feet were bleeding and my legs looked like I had been jumped on by hundreds of Birdies. The scratches stung in the sweat that was dripping down as we emerged up onto Potash Road. I didn't have a leash for Dagwood and oil tankers were known for whipping down that road just to piss off the looky-loo tourists rolling along at twenty miles per hour, so I decided it would be safest to run in the middle of the road. No car could accidentally hit him, because they'd have no problem seeing me first and slamming on the brakes. Fortunately, the stretch of road was straight, so I had a decent heads-up when a car was passing. I'd step off to the side and hold on to Dagwood's collar just to be safe.

The first two cars that passed did so slowly. But the third one stopped and rolled their window down. It was a man and a woman with a bunch of National Park pamphlets on the dash and two school-age kids in the back seat. It was then, and only then, that I remembered that I was completely topless.

Their jaws might as well have fallen through the floorboard of their rental car. I'm sure they stopped because they thought I was in danger. A half-naked woman with visibly bloodied legs running down the middle of the street? It probably looked like I had just escaped from a bunker somewhere. I doubt they were expecting my nervous laughter as I explained—completely out of breath—that my dog and I had just swam across the goddamn Colorado River. They asked if I needed a ride, which was *incredibly* kind of them given the sopping wet dog and the whole . . . half-naked thing. I declined because I was confident my plan would work, and I would rather have walked all the way back around to the bridge and through town than sit in the car with that lovely family and make small talk about their vacation.

Much to my delight, and the delight of the other dogs, my plan worked seamlessly. Dagwood and I floated leisurely downriver, making our way across, emerging back up onto the rocks like a couple of swamp creatures. Banjo lost his mind with joy at Dagwood first, of course, and then me. I lay back onto the rock to catch my breath before deciding we should get the hell out of there before anyone decided to go for another swim.

Once back in town, I went through the McDonald's drive-through for some ice cream. I parked us in a shady spot in the corner, let out a huge sigh, and stared blankly over the steering wheel while slowly licking the cone. Everything I did these days felt relatively chaotic, consistently on the verge of disastrous. A comment I read online a few days prior had said, Pathetic that she's trying to live this life she used to live with Neil. She's in over her head!

When I'd finished my ice cream, I turned to look at the dogs, who were asleep in a sopping wet pile. *We're in over our heads. . . but at least we're in*, I whispered.

chapter thirteen

The Shed

My land lay at the southernmost edge of the La Sal Mountains, where the hills taper off and flatten back out into desert valleys and canyons that roll on, red and glowing, to the south until the Abajos shoot up—seemingly out of nowhere—11,360 feet into the sky. From Up Top, I could see roughly seventy miles of wide-open, uninterrupted desert before those mountains rose up. The distance of all that glorious, wild desert is almost identical to the distance between my childhood home in Connecticut and downtown New York City. It would be like climbing up onto the roof of the little blue house I grew up in and seeing nothing but flat, rolling fields and rocks. Not one intersection, one house, one streetlamp, one building, one single light, in fact. The sparkling city skyscrapers would just jut up from ground out of nowhere like Oz. But I much preferred my view. That giant, wide-open world felt safe to me. I could see what was coming. Dust kicked up by an approaching vehicle, or the headlamp of some trespasser, or a storm slowly building in the distance. If I could see what was coming, I could prepare for it. I could keep it from catching me off guard, from ripping the roots from beneath my feet. I swore to myself that I would never let that happen again.

The storms from the Abajos would build over the range and pick up speed as they gathered the heat of the open desert, eventually slamming right into the wall of the mesa atop which the trailer sat. Meanwhile, storm clouds from the La Sals spiraled down over top of the mesa from the east. The trailer sits at just the right altitude where rain turns to hail. I was privy to both the beginning of the storms going south, and the end of the storms going north. And beginnings and endings are always the most dramatic.

We had seen our fair share of wild weather already that summer, but I was—and always will be—in awe of the storms out there. I could see them coming from miles away. Random stripes of downpouring rain swaying across the horizon like tiny tornadoes. But what took my breath away every time was the lightning. Perhaps it's how deeply purple and bruised the sky looks when you can see so much of it, but each strike seemed to have a pinkish glow around it. *Maybe it's some sort of . . . reflection of the sandstone when it hits it*, I murmured to Banjo one day, as we stood side by side in the driveway. Having no cell service meant there was no way to google these kinds of things in the moment, so I was simply left to wonder in the way we all used to. Sometimes I think it was more fun that way.

I'd watch for hours, waiting to see if they turned our way, keeping the dogs up to date with each building cloud. *One little shift in the wind, and that thing's comin' straight for us, Banj*, I'd announce. *We better go find your brother.*

My mountain bike had fallen victim to many a storm so far, since I just left it leaned up against the same juniper tree day in and day out. It was a beautiful, kitted-out bike with a bright red stripe along the frame that had been bleached by the sun, the chain rusted to a reddish-brown. It was sent to me by an outdoor retailer years back when companies were practically throwing free products at Instagrammers. From the looks of things, I wasn't exactly the golden child of that app anymore, so I didn't think there would be many more free bikes in my future. I decided I needed some way to protect this thing. Dagwood stood alongside me as I stared at the bike, hoping beyond hope that we were about to go for a ride. *Not today, bubs, I'm sorry*, I cooed. Instead, I loaded all four of them up into the Jeep and headed down to town to do some research.

Scrolling through the Lowe's and Home Depot websites via the library Wi-Fi, I was shocked to learn how much the average shed cost. Some of them could have passed for tiny homes with their quaint window shutters and vinyl siding. Others were made of solid wood and selling for as much as five thousand dollars. *Listen to this shit*, I said over my shoulder to the dogs when I climbed back into the car. I'd left it running with the AC on. *The cheapest one is this big, plastic Rubbermaid thing.* Birdie blinked back at me expectantly. *We're gonna have to assemble this thing ourselves, Beak.* It wasn't as large or nearly as heavy as most of the others, but there was still no way to have it delivered to me. Technically, I didn't even have a valid address yet, and the post office in town had a strict rule of no packages over seventy pounds. The only feasible option was to drive an hour over to Grand Junction, Colorado, to the nearest Home Depot. The fourth and final obstacle was that there wasn't a snowball's chance in hell that any shed—plastic or not—was going to fit into my Jeep. And so, much to my chagrin, I picked up my phone and called a guy I had slept with earlier that summer.

We had met in a dimly lit bar with pool tables and sticky countertops. It was one of two bars in the entire town, so you take what you can get. He was a construction worker (a different one). He had been born and raised in Moab, rode a motorcycle, and often wore leather vests without a shirt underneath. He lived in a trailer too. A lot of people in Moab live in trailers.

The first time he invited me over, we got wasted on vodka and Red Bull, and then he put on his cowboy hat and started playing a Native wooden flute. I remember being astounded at how good he was. I also remember being astounded that I was in a trailer with a flute-playing, motorcycle-riding cowboy. It was one of those moments I experienced over and over when I first moved to Moab . . . coming to in the midst of mania, looking around, and having no idea how I had gotten there.

On what I believe would be called our "second date," we spent the evening driving around, listening to country music and chatting. He was describing some new apartment complex they were putting up in Spanish Valley when he suddenly slowed the truck to a stop. "Wanna see somethin' cool?" he asked with a grin.

Ten minutes later, we pulled up to his construction site: a barren dirt lot with the early beginnings of a foundation surrounded by two massive, bright yellow bulldozers, a slew of dump trucks and forklifts, and one backhoe. "Can I?!" I asked, squealing like a toddler who'd just arrived at an amusement park. He nodded, and leaned over to give me a kiss. I had momentarily forgotten that that was sort of the premise of this whole thing, so I kissed him back quickly before throwing the door open and beelining it to the backhoe. He stood behind me, giving me a spot as I climbed the metal ladder up the side and into the driver's seat. The keys were already in it (you know . . . small-town stuff) so I cranked it and felt the whole thing shudder to life beneath me. He spent the next few minutes showing me which levers to pull, which buttons would tilt the bucket forward or backward. It might have been the best "date" I've ever been on.

The next morning, I woke up feeling excited to see him again, before realizing it wasn't really *him* I wanted to see again. *You think anyone's ever traded sex for access to heavy machinery before?* I pondered aloud to Bucket, her head resting on my shoulder from the back seat as we drove home.

He was polite, and kind, and he wanted to get to know me, so naturally, I stopped answering all of his calls and texts. I fully intended not to allow anyone to "get to know me" ever again. I intended to never let anyone get close enough to try. But he was the only one from my roster of failed dating endeavors who I could imagine spending an afternoon with without wanting to crawl out of my skin. He was also the only one with a pickup truck.

We rumbled east on I-70 past the Book Cliffs toward the Colorado border. Banjo sat on my lap, Bucket lay across the bench seat in the back, taking up more than half of it. Dagwood stood in the space she had left for him, and Birdie sat perched—like a literal bird—on the center console. He was definitely a bit put out about having to bring them along, but there was no place I could safely leave them. "They'll roast inside the trailer," I told him. "Just leave them in mine, you know I have AC," he objected. But I refused. They'd have been perfectly fine in his trailer for two hours. It was me who would not be fine. Two hours would have been the longest I'd been away from them in months. I didn't even know how to exist without them anymore. So we all piled up into the pickup, much to his chagrin.

I made a mental note to have him stop at a dispensary so I could grab some weed before we went back. I had placed the order for the shed online, so the task of picking it up was a simple one. Simple, because two guys with a forklift were waiting outside of the Home Depot and had the 330-pound box on the back of Ryan's truck in a matter of minutes. Unloading it, however, would be a different story.

When we arrived back at the property an hour or so later, the ground was practically buzzing from the midafternoon heat. The black truck bed liner burned my hands as I climbed up onto the side rail to examine the massive cardboard box. It was a seven-by-seven-foot shed with double latching doors and a slanted roof complete with plastic "shingles" and a small window that served no purpose whatsoever, but offered a nice decorative touch. I had chosen it off the website because it looked like the one my mother would have picked.

Ryan appeared as perplexed as I was about how we were going to lift this box and carry it over to the designated spot I had chosen to build it. It was wider than our wingspans in every direction and heavier than the two of us combined. I suggested he spin the truck around so the bed was facing the trailer. "And then just . . . floor it," I said, matter-of-factly. He looked at me, wide-eyed. "It's plastic, Ryan, it'll be fine." At that point, I was so desperate for him to leave, I didn't care if the thing was beat to hell before I'd even opened the box. It was genuinely disconcerting how uncomfortable I had become in the company of anyone who could speak back to me. I had grown so used to only being with the dogs, who would just look on joyfully, no matter how strange the situation in which we found ourselves. And that's exactly what they did as the pickup violently lurched forward, sending the box flying out onto the driveway with a tremendous thud. *Wooo! There it isss!* I exclaimed to them as Ryan climbed back out of the driver's seat to check the box for damages.

He made me promise to wait until his next day off to get started so he could help me build it. I recoiled at the suggestion. Gestures of caretaking no longer felt comforting. They felt like a challenge. You think I need *your* help? You think *I'm* incapable or something? I could feel my proverbial chest puff up each time.

As he pulled off down the driveway—the dogs escorting him— one of my favorite quotes from Mae West came to mind. *Every man I meet wants to protect me. I can't figure out what from.*

. . .

The moment the dust out on the road settled and I knew he was gone for certain, I rushed to the trailer to grab a knife, tearing into the box like a child on Christmas morning. The first thing I saw were clear plastic bags filled with enough screws, nails, bolts, and nuts to build one hundred IKEA dressers. In no world was I going to be able to lift that box one single inch off the ground, so I settled on carrying each and every piece, one by one, from the driveway over to the barren patch of dirt I had raked smooth. The assembly instructions very clearly stated that it should be built on a flat concrete base, but I didn't have a flat concrete base. The dirt would have to do.

For twenty minutes, I trekked back and forth. One wall. Then the other. Then the other. Then the other. One side of the roof, then the other. One side of the floor, then the other. Then two armfuls of hot metal framing and a thick paper instruction manual I carried clenched between my teeth. Standing over the pile of gray plastic and cardboard that I had successfully transported a whopping four hundred feet, I scratched my sweat-soaked scalp and muttered, *Well, fuck.*

Dagwood sat surveying the scattered contents of the box from the shade of the juniper tree he had plopped himself beneath. Each time I had dropped a piece onto the dirt, dust plumed up like smoke and settled on top of his coat, making him appear even more desert-golden than he usually did. Sometimes it was hard to tell that he *was*, in fact, getting older because his fur was rarely clean enough to see the white that had begun to appear.

I grabbed a glass of warm water from one of my blue jugs. Sitting against the shaded side of the trailer, I flipped to the first page, reading about all the suggested safety measures and materials that I, once again, did not have. I would be building this thing in a bikini top, jean shorts, Chaco sandals, and a straw cowboy hat. How else does one build a shed in the middle of nowhere on a one-hundred-degree day?

I positioned both sides of the floor in place and used my electric drill to screw them together via the four designated holes in the center. With my hands on my hips, I did a little jig on the textured plastic, and called out triumphantly to the dogs, who had all gathered beneath Dagwood's juniper by now, *Step one, DONE!*

I made it to step four before I started regretting the decision to build a shed entirely. Simply trying to get the walls to stay upright as I carried each one over to screw into the floor was impossible. Like an old black-and-white comedy film, I ran back and forth, trying to balance one wall up until I could get the other wall over to hold that one in place, but they kept collapsing like playing cards. Banjo chased me back and forth each and every time, thrilled by this new game. I could practically hear circus music in my head. Finally, I used the cooler from the deck to press up against one of the shed's walls to hold it in place as I screwed in the corner frame. Once done, I slunk to the floor beneath it. It was only midafternoon, but the sun was low enough to create a twelve-inch stretch of shade in this newly constructed corner. I chugged the rest of my—now hot—water, and stared up at the sky for a moment. There were no clouds in sight, but the wind had begun to pick up. I could feel the two plastic pieces I had just spent forty minutes trying to secure starting to sway ever so slightly. From my place on the floor, I threw both hands up and pressed them to either wall, as if anticipating its inward collapse. *I swear to God if this fucking falls . . .* I mumbled through gritted teeth.

Steps five through ten were just more seemingly futile steps to secure the paper-thin walls upright, including popping the base of each into pre-cut slots in the rubber floor. I hung off the edge of each wall, using my entire body weight, but there was no satisfying clicking sound, no puzzle piece falling into place. The plastic looked misshapen and stretched out in some places, as if the heat of some desert warehouse somewhere had warped it.

It wasn't until step fourteen that I started crying. I had already screwed in two of the metal frame pieces upside down somehow and had to undo three whole steps just to right them. But step fourteen required some tool I didn't have. Some sort of ratchet or socket or thingamabob I had no idea I'd need. *Where the fuck did it say I needed this fucking thing?* I turned toward the juniper, but all four dogs had wandered off to find something better to do. I sunk to the ground, surrounded by a sea of gray plastic and half-scattered bags of bolts. The instruction manual had long since gone from white to brown, as most any white thing out there does. I held it out in front of me, as if some invisible ink might appear, revealing that I didn't need that tool at all . . . that I could just keep powering through in a sort of frantic desperation to finish before I quit entirely.

I felt a sudden heat rising up from the pit of my stomach. I crushed the manual up between my hands and threw it—violently—to the ground in front of me. I could feel it boiling up like a teapot, the steam beginning to shake the lid. And then, it blew. I took a deep breath, gritted my teeth, and whipped around to yell at someone, to blame someone, to off-load onto someone. But there was no one. There was no one there but me.

In the wake of Dagwood's accident, my capacity to handle hard things had diminished to half its size. And it was never very big to begin with. I would upheave my frustration and my anger onto *any-one* who would listen. *Take this. Hold this. Carry this. Don't make me sit with it.* I was like a toddler who never learned to self-soothe. Anger was the muscle memory I'd clung to like a life raft since my father left when I was sixteen years old. I told myself I could let go of it someday when I felt safe. But I never let go of it.

For the first time in a long time, I was face-to-face with myself. Or perhaps, for the first time ever. I lurched forward onto all fours, suddenly convinced I was about to vomit up the half-gallon of hot water I'd chugged not long before. But what came out was nothing more than a guttural scream. Not once, in my entire life, had I felt so utterly alone. Not once had I ever felt so convinced that, perhaps, I deserved to be. The sweat streaming down from my forehead felt appropriate. It made me feel like I was struggling . . . suffering, in fact. Paying penance for something I felt like I had done wrong. Maybe it was Dagwood's accident. Maybe it was the way I'd treated Neil in the wake of it. Maybe it was what Neil had become. Maybe it was the words from an internet stranger that had echoed in my head since the day I'd read them.

I bet she was such a fucking bitch to be married to.

. . .

I sat, looking down at the dirt beneath my hands for a solid five minutes. Or maybe it was ten. I couldn't say. I had become so used to leaving my body entirely by then. The sound of the wind chime I'd hung next to my lawn chair clinked softly as the wind picked up. It always picked up in the afternoon. The crumpled-up instruction manual began to bounce across the driveway. I sprang to my feet, gasping for air, tears and spit still gurgling in the back of my throat. I lunged for it so forcefully that my fingernails cut through the dirt, leaving little half-moons of mud jammed beneath them. I held the papers to my chest, cradling them, protecting them as if they were some family heirloom I'd nearly lost. Slowly and meticulously, I pressed the pages out flat against the driveway, smoothing the creases. Wiping the snot from my face with the back of my hand, I looked over at Birdie, who was always extremely close and extremely concerned by these outbursts. *We gotta go into town, Bird. We need a . . .* I glanced down at step fourteen . . . *we need a three-eighths-inch socket wrench.*

When you come to terms with the fact that no one is coming to save you, there are really only two options. You can succumb to whatever it is that is killing you, or you can try to save yourself.

No one was coming to finish the shed. I wouldn't have dared let anyone. I needed to finish it myself, and the following day . . . I did. It took me sunup to nearly sundown in 101-degree heat, but I screwed the last hinge onto the last door just as it was dipping low enough to cast shadows. I dragged a plastic lawn chair over and sat in the shed-shaped square of shade in front of it. Canned margarita in hand, I slid back onto the warm white plastic and gazed up at my work. It was most certainly lopsided, and some little creature must have already made a home beneath it since Bucket stood watch over where Banjo had begun to dig furiously. But it was finished. And I had finished it. I had no one to blame, and only myself to thank.

I documented this whole process on my Instagram, of course, but I never let on how much this shed *was* actually killing me that first day. Killing some old version of me. Peeling away some too-tight skin I was ready to shed. A woman responded to one of my videos in which I successfully carried a piece of the seven-foot roof up the ladder.

It feels like you're building this shed for women everywhere.

Perhaps I had been more transparent than I'd thought. Perhaps most people knew that it wasn't really about the shed anymore. It was bigger. It was about coming to terms with who I had been, and who I had no choice but to be now: as if I was being dragged—kicking and screaming—into the person I'd become. Someone who could take care of herself. Someone who could learn to forgive herself for those times when she didn't know how.

The lightning started out silent at first. It started even before the rain did. Only a few relatively dry weeks had passed since I had put the shed up, but monsoon season crept up as fast as the storm overhead had. The days were still in the triple digits. It had barely dropped below eighty-five degrees the night before. I drifted in and out of a sweat-soaked sleep, the solar power charging my box fan having run out hours ago. Without warning, a crash of thunder louder than any I had ever heard exploded from the sky. It shook the ground. It felt like it shook my ribcage. I shot up and pulled back the curtains just in time to see a three-pronged lightning strike hit the ground beyond the dirt road. I scrambled from the bed and ran outside, the screen door slapping loudly behind me. I had never seen a storm this big, a sky this dark so early in the morning. It looked like something out of a sci-fi movie. I half expected some sort of alien ship to descend from the center of it. What was even more eerie was the complete and utter lack of wind. The wind chime on the juniper beside the deck hung perfectly still.

As much as I could have stood out there and watched it until it was right on top of us, I had to make sure we were all tucked inside the trailer far sooner. Dagwood had hated the sound of thunder ever since a coal truck—parked less than one hundred yards from Bertha—was struck by lightning during one such summer storm many years ago.

I ran back into the trailer, ushering the dogs in one by one. Dagwood jumped up onto the bed, where I covered him with as many pillows as I could find. The weight seemed to comfort him. I barely had time to crank the windows closed before the big fat raindrops started splattering against them. Rain in the desert pools long before it absorbs. Anything loose blows away, leaving only tightly packed soil and smooth rock. Sudden bouts of heavy rainfall on earth like that is akin to pouring water onto concrete. In a matter of minutes, it begins to roll downward, gathering speed, carving little pathways through the sand that look like river tributaries from a plane window. Those tributaries funnel that ever-increasing water into the larger washes. Some of those washes are as wide as roadways, and it takes only one bad storm to fill them entirely. Catastrophic floods that began as a few raindrops.

I watched from the window as the muddy, terra-cotta water flowed down beside the driveway and through the drainage pipe that had been buried beneath it. It was only when the water crested the top of the driveway that I began to worry. When it started rushing over the top of it with enough strength to push rocks that wouldn't fit in my palm, I decided it was time to get in the car. I threw a few things of value into a canvas bag in case the trailer washed away entirely. My turquoise jewelry. My electronics. A picture of my grandmother smoking a cigarette, shotgun in hand.

Just before we made a run for it, there were sudden popping sounds on the roof. Birdie nearly jumped out of her skin at the deafening sound. It felt like the trailer was being shot with BB guns. I cracked the door open to find hail that was apparently big enough to break windows. I had forgotten to close a small one near the front door. The tiny, horizontal plate of glass had splintered down the middle. I took a deep breath and looked down at the dogs who had gathered around me, noses flush to the trailer door. *Ready? One. Two. Three!* We burst outside into the pounding hail. I donkey-kicked the door closed from behind me while covering my head with one hand

and holding tight to Dagwood's collar with the other. All five of us piled up into the Jeep, more bruised than we were wet. I winced at the sound of the hail on the windshield, holding my breath, expecting that to shatter at any second too.

I paused before driving over the two large culverts buried beneath the bottom section of the driveway. It was essentially a bridge made of dirt. It had been packed up high and pressed down tight, but I didn't have much confidence that it would hold. I debated which side I would rather be stuck on if the water took it out completely. *Maybe we should stay in the trailer?* I mused aloud to the dogs. Dagwood was panting rapidly behind me, as he did when he was stressed. I had to get him away from the storm.

As I drove down the sloping switchbacks toward town, I realized my tires were sliding, not spinning. If I went off the road to the left, we'd be stuck in what was once a drainage ditch, but was now a small river of rocks. If we slid off the road to the right, we would go straight off a cliff, two hundred feet down to Highway 191. I pumped the brakes as gently as possible, holding my breath. *Please please please please* I chanted aloud, death-gripping the steering wheel. The farther down the hill we slid, the quieter it got. The hail returned to rain, flowing down over the rocks like a chocolate fountain. By the time the tires touched pavement, a rainbow had appeared, vivid against the still-purple storm clouds that swirled above the mesa like a haunted castle. I sat silently, watching the sky lighten up, the wind slowly carry the clouds away. Dagwood still lay curled in as tight a ball as he could get into, given that he couldn't quite bend his bad leg. Bucket and Birdie stared at me, wide-eyed, heads tucked low to get as far away from the beating of water on the roof as possible. Banjo, of course, was fast asleep.

I returned to the mesa later that afternoon, precariously driving back up the switchbacks, my chaotic tire tracks still visible in the slowly drying mud. The sun was out, the sky a cerulean blue. I stood on the dirt road surveying The Wash, which had become a full-blown river. A river surely strong enough to sweep myself (and most certainly the dogs) beneath the churning debris it carried toward the next culvert beneath the main road. They whined from inside the car until I pointed at them through the half-cracked window. *Stay.*

The driveway had nearly been washed out completely, the soil ripped out from one of the juniper trees beside it, leaving its roots protruding out like spider legs. The Jeep violently bounced over what was left of it. I had to keep my speed up so as not to get caught in the mud. When we reached the top of the driveway, I was relieved to see that the trailer was unmoved. And I was surprisingly at peace when I peered behind it to find that the shed had been absolutely demolished. The floor had physically slid out from the rushing of water and mud, leaving the collapsed walls a few feet behind it. I'm sure that's why the instructions were firm about building it on concrete. The walls had collapsed inward, at least, which created a haphazard tepee that had provided at least some protection for the shed's contents. All five of us gathered around it, staring solemnly, as if watching a casket being lowered into the ground. *Well . . .* I said, *I guess that's that.*

Mother Nature is a mess sometimes. It's as if she just doesn't know what to do with herself. She's hot sometimes, cold at others. She boasts smooth meadows right beside jagged mountains. There is silence and cacophony, all existing simultaneously within her. Exquisite and complicated. A rainbow in the middle of a brutal storm.

The earth itself and all the beautiful things we love about it are direct results of violent volcanic eruptions. Our very existence is the result of what can only be described as *a bang*. Sometimes there needs to be a great rumbling, an explosion, a brutal disaster, before the next beautiful thing can be made. Nature has always seemed quite human to me in that way.

chapter fourteen

Politician's Think Tank

In the desert, you usually hear the wind long before you feel it. There's not much to be blown about out there, no towering trees to sway, their leaves rattling like instruments. The wind just builds and builds across miles of open sky, uninterrupted until the roar of it rushes past your ears, covers your skin with a fine layer of sand. I mistook the wind for a lot of things out there. Most often, an approaching car, a stranger passing through. A stranger who had found one of my hiding places. But strangers never came. Only the wind.

The dogs would lift their chins ever so slightly at the sound of its approach, wrinkled noses twitching side to side, eyes squinted like half-moons, reveling in the new scent of some far-off thing. *How many muscles are in a dog's nose?* I wonder. When you lie around in the desert waiting for the sound of the wind, you have the privilege of wondering about little things like that. The privilege of watching the tiny legs of black flies skitter across my freckles, their straw-like mouthpiece pressed to the flesh. If I waved them off one limb, they'd just bounce to another, so it was best to breathe through it . . . to try to ignore it. I treated it as a kind of meditation. A practice in discomfort.

"Those things land on cow shit, you know," Mary said to me, as she swatted them from her own legs one afternoon. I smirked, thinking of how many times my dogs had picked up cow shit, how many seemingly foul things had been in their mouths prior to licking my face. And yet, I'd go years without so much as a stomach bug or a common cold. I chalk it up to an immune system carved from desert dirt, black flies, and cow shit. Sometimes I forgot I wasn't a dog until other people were around, until they started pointing out things that I'd stopped considering a very long time ago.

Mary had flown back out for a visit that I intended to make far more fun than her last one. "There will be no legal proceedings," I joked when she got in the car. Having flown in from New Orleans, the dry heat was a relief to her, despite the forecast calling for triple digits that afternoon. We rolled south from the airport, stopping in town to get some groceries, before continuing to The Property.

The tourist part of town lasts for approximately one mile before it melts back off into locals' territory. Auto repair shops, dilapidated trailer parks, and dirt lots full of construction equipment frame either side of 191, interrupted every now and again by big, sparkly billboards about jumping out of an airplane or crashing through rapids on the Colorado River. Each one displayed a GoPro photo of some tourist in absolute euphoria and/or total terror. From a marketing standpoint, I'm sure these were intentionally indistinguishable. Moab is where people come to feel *alive . . .* to feel as though they're doing something truly *dangerous*, despite the fact that statistics deem them more likely to die in a car accident on the way there in the first place. I like to hope that people leave a place like Moab with the mental souvenir that it's far more dangerous to have never really lived at all.

The closer we got to the turnoff onto my road, the more I found myself glancing over at Mary. So much so that she requested I *keep my eyes on the road, for Christ's sake.* I think she worried there was still a chance I might snap and just Thelma-and-Louise-style floor it off a cliff in a blaze of glory. But I just wanted to see her seeing all of this. I wanted to know I wasn't overreacting, because there had seldom been a time that I didn't shed a tear of joy on my way home from the grocery store.

Mostly, I wanted to see it through someone else's eyes so I knew it was real. Mentally, it felt as though I was still weaving in and out of reality. There were weeks—entire months, even—that were missing from my memory of the year before. I'd always been familiar with the effects of mental illness, having dealt with depression since I was in high school. But the symptoms of my depression never made me feel *ashamed*, and they most certainly never made me feel *crazy*. But in the wake of the divorce and the relentless online harassment (all in the midst of an unprecedented global pandemic, I might add), I left my own body in a way I didn't even know was possible. I was in the car, but I was no longer driving. I was going through the motions of being alive, but nothing felt real. Conversations didn't feel real. Consequences didn't feel real. *Nothing* felt real.

My psychiatrist had been dead-on with the mania diagnosis. I was truly textbook. The process of returning to my body in the months that followed was a painstakingly slow one. I was no longer safe in my delusions, no longer able to slip into them with such ease. Perhaps it sounds odd, but there were so many nights alone in the trailer that I missed the ability to just . . . go somewhere else for a little while. But I was making progress, and I wanted Mary to see that. I wanted her to see this person I was becoming.

When I turned down the driveway, she gasped. "I'm so proud of you, Bri. Oh my god. This is *yours*. This is *real*." It was almost as if she could hear my inner dialogue. Old friends are good at that.

We were greeted at the top of the driveway by Banjo, lounging on a dirt mound in front of the trailer in the early morning sun. This would now be the third time that he burst through the screen window above the couch, despite my replacing it with heavy-duty screen, a screen that promised to withstand the clawing of the family cats and dogs. The problem is that Banjo didn't *use* his claws. Instead, he would get a running start and dive through it like a stuntman in an action film. In the screen's defense, it really *didn't* rip. It just burst forth from the thin metal frame in one big piece.

"Why don't you just close the windows?" Mary asked, bending down to greet him as he wriggled toward us, thrilled to see us, but knowing I was less than thrilled to see him at the moment.

"I told you; I don't have any air conditioning." *What the fuck, Banjo?!* I bent over with my hands on my hips. *No! NO! How many times have I told you this?! You can't jump out the window!* He stood there, looking up at me slack-jawed, tail wagging. We both knew he would most certainly continue jumping out the windows.

The other three howled from inside the trailer, surely jealous beyond measure. The moment the door opened, they sprinted to Mary, who was already struggling with those completely impractical suitcases she had brought again. *Okay ... okay ... okay! OKAY! Off! OFF! Heel! Heel! Birdie, HEEL! Off!!* Mary loved dogs, but being nearly tackled by four of them at once would be a lot for anyone. As I helped gently shoo them away, I made a mental note that I might eventually have to teach Birdie and Banjo what those commands meant. Bucket and Dagwood were a lost cause, and had most certainly entered the age range in which they should be allowed to do what they wanted anyway. Just like the old folks who blurt out whatever inappropriate thing comes to mind. The grandkids just roll their eyes and shrug, *Ain't no changin' 'em now.*

I had planned a litany of activities for Mary and me so that this trip would feel more like a vacation. It wasn't until she asked for the bathroom that I realized this might not be what most people envision when they think of a vacation. "Number one or number two?" I asked, tossing her bags up onto the porch. "Number one is just kinda, ya know, go anywhere," I said, gesturing to the sand around us, "but number two requires a bit more effort . . ."

"Y-you still don't have a bathroom??" she stammered, incredulously.

"Is it an emergency?" I asked.

We stood there in a stalemate for a minute before she finally said, "It's number one."

I watched her round a nearby bush, shaking her head while unbuttoning her shorts. It hadn't really occurred to me that not everyone pees in the bushes all day every day. It wasn't until I'd asked another person to live my life that I realized just how strange my life had become.

"There's a bathroom right there!" Mary exclaimed as she stepped into the trailer, pointing at what was, indeed, a bathroom.

"It's still broken," I said. "Actually, it never really worked in the first place."

I kicked a pile of clothes aside as I guided her down the hallway toward the bed. There was no way to get around each other in the hallway other than to basically hug and spin. Dog hair floated around as if inside a snow globe. It stuck to the sweat on our shoulders.

"What do you think?" I asked, as Banjo leapt onto the bed, furiously licking Mary's face the moment she lay down.

"It's cute in here!" She smiled, nervously. "Hotter than hell, though . . ."

"Yeah you can't spend much time *inside* the trailer once the sun comes up," I laughed. "Tomorrow, I'm taking us on an adventure to go find some water."

That night, we ate some plastic containers of pre-made salad I'd purchased in town. Mary seemed to be keeping track of each bite I took, which was probably one for every five sips of wine. Mary pointed to my knees as I sat cross-legged on the couch beside her. They were covered in bruises that looked more green and yellow than black and blue. "I bruise easily," I said. "I think I need to take B vitamins or something."

"I think you need to eat more food, Brianna," she said, sternly. I lifted a fork full of lettuce to my mouth, chewing dramatically in her direction like a toddler would.

The following morning, I loaded the Jeep up with a tent, backpacks, and the extra sleeping bag and sleeping pad I had bought for Mary last minute. I was still used to owning all my gear in sets of two. As we drove north toward town, Mary detailed the difficult night of sleep she'd had. "Banjo slept with his body sprawled across my chest and I got up to go pee but damn near fell out the door because I didn't want to wake you up with my phone flashlight."

"Did you see the stars though?!" I gasped.

She perked up. "Oh my God, yes. Incredible! The Milky Way was across the entire sky. I don't think I've ever seen that many stars."

"You'll probably see even more tonight if it stays clear like it's been." I smiled. *She saw our stars, Bird!!* I squealed to Birdie, who had thrust her head over my shoulder from the back seat.

Several hours later, I turned the Jeep left off of Highway 24 and shifted into four-wheel drive. "You ready?" I asked excitedly. "We've got eleven-ish miles on this dirt road and then you're just kinda drivin' in a wash. We'll just have to wait to see if it's flooded and decide whether we wanna risk crossing it by car or on foot. The Jeep's tires are pretty solid . . ." Mary stared blankly at me as I trailed off in thought. Despite being the best of friends, an extreme passion for the outdoors was not something we shared. Mary was entirely unfamiliar with dirt roads, and she was most certainly not familiar with driving on something that couldn't even be called a road. She braced herself with outstretched arms against the passenger door and the center console as the obstacles I drove us over got bigger and bigger. When our tire temporarily sunk into some deep sand, Mary looked on nervously from the open passenger window as I dug us out.

"Bri, we are, like, way the hell out here, where is the nearest town right now even?"

"We're fiiiinneee, Marryyyy," I said, soft and sing-songy, as one might do when comforting a child. With each bump, each rock, each rustle in the sagebrush, I uttered it over and over again, just like I did to myself all the time. *We're fine. It's fine. We're fine.*

I set up our tent on a flat patch of sand across a dried river that opened up into a slot canyon. "Normally you wouldn't want to set up right here because if there was ever a flash flood, you'd just be right in it," I joked, "but I checked the weather. It's fine." Mary rolled her eyes, but was too excited to go exploring so she didn't fight me on it. We wandered up the road a little way toward a spring I'd been to once before. "You can drink the water right from the bottom of the sandstone. It's the most filtered water you'll ever have!" I said.

"Yeah, I won't be doing that," she said back, flatly. The spring was nothing magnificent. In fact, it was just sort of a permanent puddle that kept a section of the dirt road consistently washed out. The eruption of green plants all along the perimeter was the only giveaway that this wasn't just leftover rainwater. We picked the deepest spot—probably eight inches at best—and sat with our butts in the water, toes out straight in front of us like a couple of lanky kids in the shallow end of the pool. "Quit layin' around eatin' bonbons down there!" our old swim coach used to yell at us. We laughed, watching the dogs run amok all around us in the fading sunlight.

"I'm worried about you, Bri," Mary said suddenly.

"What?" I laughed, "Just this morning you said you were proud of me!"

But Mary wasn't laughing. In fact, she had started to cry.

"I'm fine, Mary," I sighed. I figured she was talking about my gaunt face and protruding collarbones, or perhaps the cooler full of alcohol I kept in close proximity at all times. I was surprised when she turned to face me, shouting, "Why don't you have a fucking toilet, Bri?! Why won't you just get the toilet fixed? You can afford it! Just fix the toilet. Find someone who can fix it!"

I laughed, uncertain whether or not she was really serious. "It doesn't matter to me, Mary, it's fine. I'm fi—"

She cut me off. "YOU ARE NOT FUCKING FINE, BRI! This isn't normal." The sheer force of her voice startled me. It seemed to startle everything out there. The wind died. I could have sworn the birdsong cut out like a record scratch.

I raged back at her, matching her volume now. "This is normal for *me*!" I yelled, fervently guarding my rock bottom with every ounce of strength I had.

"Why are you doing this to yourself? You look like you weigh ninety pounds. You're alone all day, every day, day after day."

"That's not true, I have the dogs!" I interjected.

"So, you and the dogs? That's all it's ever gonna be?"

"And you." I smiled, but she didn't smile back.

"Why are you making things so much harder than they need to be? What are you blaming yourself for? Neil?? You couldn't have fixed him, Bri. You couldn't have saved him. All you could do was save yourself."

She scooched her butt closer through the sand and wrapped her arms around me, cradling the back of my head with her hands. I could think of nothing to say, so I just wept.

I lay in the tent that night, wide awake, staring at the stars while Mary slept beside me. I had pulled out the trailer manual one time shortly after I had bought it. That toilet was the same year as the trailer itself, which meant the manual that came with it was thirty-eight years old. Its pages were ripped and urine-yellow like Bertha's manual had been. I had basically been using the trailer the same way I had used Bertha, so I tossed that manual aside too, never bothering to read it.

I had no expectation of running water or a working toilet or a way to control the temperature. Bertha was just a metal shell I lived inside of, and now the trailer was just a bigger metal shell that I could actually stand up in. That was good enough for me. I was used to being outside, being dirty and messy and rugged and carefree. I was used to making the most of what I had. But the fact is, I *had* a toilet. I *had* a sink and a shower and enough propane to power the heater if I ever bothered to get it fixed. I just didn't care enough to get it fixed because I had stopped caring about anything. My depression tricked me into believing I didn't deserve nice things, even the most basic things. *Look what happened to Neil. Look what happened to Dagwood. Look what happened to your friends just for being associated with you. Look at the wake of destruction you've left.*

I started to cry, cupping my hand to my mouth, so as not to wake Mary. I didn't want her knowing how right she was. I was drinking myself to sleep, starving myself to a silhouette, and living in a relative state of squalor simply because it felt like that's what I deserved. The desert, these dogs, the manual labor, the sweat, the blood, the freezing cold, the way nothing—and I mean *nothing*—was simple . . . those were the only things that made me feel accomplished, made me feel like I was doing anything right. In every other area of my life, I was weak and broken and beaten. I had lost, failed, lied, made a fool of myself. I had found the perfect place out in the desert to build my tower, and I had successfully locked myself in it. One would think I'd have a pretty good view from up there, but all I could see was myself. I let every message wound me. Every comment cut bone-deep. I believed what people said. Strangers. Neil. His family. I believed all of it. It must have been true, after all. No one goes to *those* lengths unless someone is really, really bad. *I must be really, really bad.* I must deserve nothing.

Mary reached over and gently squeezed my hand. I squeezed it back twice.

Fixing all those wounded parts of me was going to take time, and I knew that. I dreaded that. But the toilet seemed like something that might only take an afternoon, so it seemed like a good place to start.

Two weeks after Mary left, I spent the morning pacing back and forth across the driveway, glancing down every two minutes toward the place where the road met the sky. Cars drove past so rarely up there that the sound of one was genuinely startling. Instinctively, all five of us would freeze, eyes and ears tilted toward the rumbling. Holding my breath, I'd peer around the trailer or whatever dead juniper tree I'd been sawing down, but all that was actually visible was the dust kicked up by the tires.

More often than not, it was just the UPS truck. It didn't happen every day, but if it did, it was between the hours of 1:00 and 3:00 p.m. The sound was unmistakable; the cloud of dust that followed, even more so. I'd jump up from whatever I was doing—which, most of the time, was nothing—and yell to the dogs, excitedly, *He's here! C'mon let's go!* The five of us would sprint up to one of the biggest boulders on the trail to Up Top. We had a perfect view of the road from there. It sounds more like a gang of kids waiting on the ice cream truck than a woman watching a UPS truck drive by, but I'd never seen a truck *that* size going *that* fast down a dirt road. It looked positively unruly. He was Jeff Gordan behind the wheel. The big boxy front grill of the truck looked like something out of *Mad Max* with all that kicked up dust. I'd sit, grinning ear to ear, as he flew by, engine roaring, tires kicking up rocks. He must have been having the time of his life out there going a few dozen miles per hour over the speed limit, but who was I to stop him. He probably thought he was alone on that stretch of road too. After all, my trailer wasn't even visible from out there. It was barely ten feet high and tucked eight hundred feet back beyond the tallest junipers.

My suspicions were confirmed that day when I watched, perched on top of that same boulder, as a large white septic truck came to a steaming halt in the middle of the road just shy of my driveway. It sat idling out in the road for a solid two minutes. I crouched behind a bush like an animal, debating whether or not to walk down there. Banjo and Birdie crouched on either side of me, vigilant, ready to charge toward whatever it was we were going to be charging toward. Details never mattered much to them.

I turned to face Banjo, who looked back at me with his wide, brown eyes. *The toilet guy's here, Banj. Should we escort him up?* And escort him up they did. I only had to walk halfway down the driveway with my arm waving before he spotted me and shifted into gear again. The dogs, however, went careening, barking wildly at this beast of a truck that was slowly rolling toward us all. I called them back, but didn't scold them. Barking at strangers on our property was something I had no intention of training out of them.

After realizing that this was someone I was expecting, the dogs pranced in front of the truck's massive front end, guiding it slowly up to the trailer. As I walked ahead of them all, I felt a rush of fear. *What if he knows who I am? What if he follows me on Instagram? What if he's heard about me from people in town?*

I wracked my brain, trying to find anything in the mess of memories I'd managed to make about people I had met in this town. The woman at the farm and feed store had given me this guy's business card after I had somehow worked my lack of toilet into conversation at the checkout counter. It doesn't take much isolation to send a person's social cues off the deep end, apparently. My paranoia seemed to have gone off the deep end as well. Perhaps it all sounds far-fetched, but I had decided that anything was possible the day my address was posted on Reddit.

The first thing I realized the moment he stepped down from the driver's seat was that he did *not* follow me on Instagram. He very likely didn't even *have* Instagram. The second thing I realized was that he wasn't wearing any shoes. He was white-haired with skin that had tanned to hide. I cannot speak to whether this is true of his beliefs, but his physical appearance was straight out of the movie *Deliverance*. He donned a pair of jeans, a brown belt, and a T-shirt that was likely sold as "white" but could be described now as yellow, at best. But no shoes. In fact, it didn't look like he'd worn shoes a day in his whole life. The cracks in his heels were black and curling up the sides of his feet like vines stretching toward the sky. He had more toes missing nails than toes that were not. Banjo charged in, nibbling them the way he would nibble on my ears in the morning. *Quit corn-cobbin' me*, I'd laugh, playfully swatting him away. The toilet man didn't swat Banjo away, but he also didn't acknowledge him at all. He didn't acknowledge any of the dogs, in fact, despite their inconsolable joy at his arrival. *Banjo, quit!* I said from behind gritted teeth. Bucket had been nuzzling her head against his leg, but stormed off soon after realizing he wasn't going to be doling out any scratches.

"What do we got goin' on out here?" he said, his hands on his hips, surveying the surroundings like a sheriff in an old Western town. I looked beyond his shoulder at the white septic tank on the back of his truck. In big, black letters printed on the side, it read, POLITICIAN'S THINK TANK.

"The toilet's broken," I said in a hushed voice, as though I would be in trouble at this admission.

"Mmmhmm, broken like how?" he asked, still looking all around at the horizon instead of at any of us.

"Well, I haven't ever had it working in the first place. I think there's a crack in the holding tank. Anything that went in seemed to seep out. Only took me a few hours to realize it wasn't usable. So it's just been kinda sittin' like that ever since . . ."

"Mmmhhmm," he said, like a man who's somehow heard a woman tell this very specific story forty times. "Probably got a crack in your tank." I held a finger up to assert that I had *just* said that, but decided it wasn't worth the effort. He stepped up onto the deck and into the trailer, the dogs following his every move. It was alarming to have a stranger in there. It made it look so small, so make-believe, as if a child had asked her grandfather to come fix her dollhouse.

I couldn't keep my eyes off his feet as he got down onto his knees to shove his face into the toilet. Banjo stood alongside him, eye-level, tail wagging, looking into the toilet as though he had been hired as an assistant. "Well, there's a bunch of toilet paper and shit down in that tank that has dried damn near to cement," he shouted, directly into the toilet. Banjo turned to look at me as if to say, *See, Ma, that's what I've been sayin'!*

He stood to face me, still not acknowledging Banjo's efforts in the slightest. "You gotta seal that crack up, first and foremost, but I don't do that kinda thing. I don't know all that much about trailers, to be honest, people just give my name out when someone's got a shit problem." Looking at him dead-on now, I could see he had a lip full of tobacco.

He went on to explain that the "concrete block of shit from the nineties" would need to be "rehydrated." He motioned toward my blue water jug with one of his bare feet. "You got more'a those?" I nodded. "Good, good. You're gonna need 'em." He shuffled past me and back out onto the porch. "You patch that crack," he said, "and we can get that sucked right outta there." He made a whooshing sound, which really added to whatever horrifying visuals I had already conjured. He said he'd be back the following week, and then he was gone like a fever dream. The behemoth truck dwarfing the trailer seemed like it hadn't even been there at all the moment he rounded the last stretch of road. *What a character, huh?* I said to Dags, as he stood beside me.

As amusing as the encounter had been, I did not feel the need to invite any additional repairmen to my trailer. I resolved to fix the crack in the tank myself. At the hardware store in town, I bought a drop cloth, a box of latex gloves, and a tube of that flexible glue stuff that you see on the infomercials. I recalled the man ranting about how *incredible!* it was while floating in a rowboat he claimed he had fixed it with.

Back at the trailer, I laid the cloth down, tied a bandana over my face, slipped on some gloves, and shimmied beneath it. I lay on my back, the tank less than a foot away from my face. I tried not to breathe through my nose. The crack was clearly visible, but the contents of the tank were "cement" so nothing dripped from inside of it. I dragged the tube of glue along the surface, using a gloved finger to push the extra goop farther up inside. I used the entire bottle, just for good measure, although the end result looked a bit like some gelatinous mold was now growing out from the crack instead.

I spent the glue's suggested drying time mentally preparing myself for the next step. I'd filled three of my five-gallon blue jugs with water from town. The septic guy said I'd need to pour as much water as I could straight down into the tank through the toilet. If the crack was fixed, the water would sit in there and rehydrate all the old toilet paper. "You want it to get *real* soupy if we're gonna get it out," I recalled him saying. I poured a gallon or so of water into the toilet before running outside and crouching beside the tank where the clear glue had dried to a milky white. I held my breath, waiting to see if anything dripped through. It held. *It held!* I shouted.

By the time the dogs escorted the Politician's Think Tank back down the driveway a few days later, I had poured almost twenty gallons of water into the tank. The man stepped down from the front seat barefoot, unsurprisingly. "There's gotta be almost twenty gallons in there now," I said proudly.

Banjo clocked in immediately, tail wagging, following him back and forth as he connected the large, clear hose from the tank to his truck. It sounded like any other vacuum when he finally turned it on, but things didn't "suck right out" the way I was anticipating. He stood over the hose, watching sparse amounts of liquid pass through, shaking his head in disappointment. He shouted something at me.

"What?" I yelled. He walked back to the truck to turn the pump off.

"Did you stir it?" he said, apparently for the second time. The look of horror on my face answered the question for him. "You *gotta* stir it up," he muttered, rolling his eyes, as if rehydrating decades-old toilet paper were a basic life skill. He opened his passenger door and rooted around behind the seat until he came up with a long piece of metal rebar in hand. To spare you the full details, just envision a barefoot man in an Allman Brothers T-shirt churning butter in my toilet with a piece of rebar. I stood watching, eyebrows still raised in shock. After what seemed like far too long, he walked back out to the truck and flipped the pump on again. Immediately, the contents of the trailer's tank started flowing right up into the politician's tank.

Shortly after he'd left, I stepped back into the trailer to find that he had left the piece of rebar sticking up out of the toilet like a cocktail umbrella. I texted a photo of it to Mary. Toilet's fixed!

chapter fifteen

Baja

I decided to go to Mexico six hours after I started driving to Mexico. That is to say, I could have chickened out and picked a myriad of different destinations along the way to claim as my final one and none would have been the wiser. Southern California, or some sand dune in New Mexico, or, perhaps, the Superstition Mountains in Arizona where it's rumored that author Edward Abbey's body is buried. As the story goes, shortly after he died, a few of his old, gray-haired buddies loaded his body up into the back of a pickup truck. Word of such a notable person's death would spread quickly, so they didn't have much time. They drove deep into the Superstition Mountains and buried him somewhere out there in an unmarked grave. Buried him so good, no one's ever found him. This was all a part of Ed's plan, mind you. He had left these very instructions as his dying wish. It's illegal to go out burying human bodies in the desert, but of course, Ed knew that too. He didn't like authority or the rules they invented. He thought that deserts should be left wild, that all roads should remain dirt, and that he had every right to die and turn to dust out there like any other animal. One final, everlasting *fuck you*.

I sat in my idling car at a Podunk gas station outside Phoenix, Arizona, examining the map on my phone. If I headed east, I'd be in the Superstition Mountains in three hours. If I continued south, I'd hit the Mexican border in four. *We could go hang out with Ed*, I mused aloud to the dogs. Chewing the inside of my lip, I turned to face them. Four sets of eyes transfixed on mine. I closed the GPS, turned the music up, and steered us south.

Ed would have driven to Mexico.

I can tell you with absolute certainty that this is my mother's least favorite thing I have ever done. It didn't exactly shock her, though, as not much does anymore. People—both in my real life and on the internet—were so worried that I was going to be murdered or injured or stranded somewhere without cell service, left to die and be picked apart by vultures. But as callous as it sounds, I'd read a few of those comments, shrug, and mumble, *If I die, I die, I guess.*

This is a mindset I'd had long before the deep depression that followed my divorce, and it was a mindset completely opposite of my recent bout of suicidal ideation. Perhaps that sounds odd, given that dying is dying . . . but if you want to *stay* alive, it's presumably because you want to *live*. And yet, when presented with all kinds of opportunities for travel or adventure or thrill, folks shrivel backward into the corner, writhing their hands in discomfort, avoiding eye contact with that opportunity at all costs. *Oh, me? I could never. What if something horrible happens? What if I die?* I've never really understood the concept of not doing something adventurous because you might die. I'm not quite sure what people are saving themselves for. It's as though they see life as a competition to survive, with the prize being . . . death? *At least you won't have any scars when they lower your body into the ground.*

It has always been very simple for me. I'm not so sure there is a "point" to life, but if there is, I'm certain it is not to preserve ourselves for death. We hear it all the time. Some old man dies, surrounded by loved ones—his final piece of advice being to do more, love more, see more, worry less. And yet, so many of us don't seem to *hear* that at all.

This obsession I had with living while being alive has fostered a sort of . . . spontaneous decisiveness . . . which is an interesting combination. I will often decide to do something out of the blue, and then become so feverishly committed, so bone-deep decided on this sudden idea that one would think I had been planning it for months. Once the initial rush subsides, the reality sets in, but only *after* these decisions have already been made . . . after the bank account has been drained for a rusted orange van . . . after the ink has dried on the title for an undeveloped nine-acre plot of land . . . after I'm already sitting, alone, in a long line of cars at the Mexican border with four dogs' heads sprouting from the open windows.

It was almost August. The heat rose off the pavement, swirling up and mixing in with hundreds of idling car engines in a near-visible steam. The air was so thick, you could choke on it. The last time I crossed the Mexican border, Bertha had died directly in the customs stall. Front wheels in Mexico, back wheels in the United States. I had been with Neil then, so things didn't feel so nerve-wracking. (Mind you, I never said I wasn't nervous just because I was decisive.)

Two Border Patrol officers approached my car as I fumbled for my passport. The passport I'd had over twenty minutes to get out of my bag while waiting in line. But I had spent the entirety of that time on the phone with my mother, who was reminding me that it wasn't too late to go to the Superstition Mountains. She demanded that I call her right before I crossed the border. She seemed to think it was some portal into another galaxy that I would get sucked into as soon as the stamp hit my passport.

The dogs barked at the two officers who stood on either side of my front windows. I had stopped discouraging them from doing that because it's a pretty quick way to let passersby know that this woman isn't technically *alone*. One officer plucked the passport from my hand while the other leaned in through the open passenger window, examining the contents on the seat, and the jumbo-size bag of dog food shoved down onto the floormat. It was so heavy that if I put it *on* the front seat, the car would register it as a person who was not wearing their seat belt. With a glance and a stamp, they waved me onward into the streets of Mexicali. I put Grateful Dead's "Mexicali Blues" on the stereo and rolled the windows back down. It was scorching hot, but I wanted every single sense to take it in.

I had driven this stretch of road before, on that almost-failed attempt to cross the border with Neil. I've always been good with directions, but I was still slightly surprised to find that things looked familiar to me after so much time had passed. At a stoplight up ahead, I recognized the man standing between the waiting cars, juggling flaming bowling pins. *Holy shit, Buck, he's still here!* Bucket pressed her face to the side of mine, as if to lean past me to see for herself. *God, it's been like . . . four years.* I suppose it could have been a different guy now, but I can't imagine there's a surplus of local fire jugglers around. I waved as the light turned green, and he flashed me a toothy, yellow smile.

Once I passed the huge, crashed airplane that had somehow ended up on the left side of the road, it was straight out onto Route 1. Driving in Baja couldn't be easier. There are two roads that take you all the way down the peninsula. Route 1 along the Sea of Cortez side, and Route 5 along the Gulf of California. They both begin at the border and split off immediately to the east and west. At no point do they meet again until the bottom of the peninsula; at least, not on any road you wouldn't need some serious four-wheel drive for. You take the 1 down or you take the 5 down. If you can drive in a straight line, you can navigate Baja.

I pulled into San Felipe just as the sun began to sink. It's the first town that crops up after miles of salt flats and desert dust, and is populated by a seemingly even split of local Mexicans and old white people. I wasn't sure I would have any sort of service, so I had taken dozens and dozens of screenshots before I left the States.

I scrolled through, looking for the check-in instructions for my Airbnb. I planned to stay in Airbnbs the entire time because it was

July and sleeping in a tent with four dogs would be a sauna. My mom also felt better knowing I was in any sort of structure that had locking doors. The plus side of being there in July was that no one else really was, which means the Airbnbs were cheap. As I pulled the Jeep up into the gated driveway of a four-bedroom white stucco mansion, I laughed aloud. *We paid fifty-three US dollars for this place, you guys.*

My plan was to use the Wi-Fi at one Airbnb to book the next Airbnb, and so on and so forth as I made my way down the peninsula. But having nothing booked in advance meant I could stay extra days in a town I particularly liked, or meander off to a town I hadn't even heard of yet. All my reservations were intentionally last minute. Just in case I lost track of time on purpose.

The following morning, I made myself a cup of instant coffee. The host was kind enough to place the plastic packet in a ceramic mug along with a plastic spoon. The dogs wandered around the stone courtyard for a while until I had to open the gate and let them out into the dirt patch across the road. They seemed completely baffled at the concept of going to the bathroom on concrete. It was a beautiful house, but I was itching to get going. The farther I was from the border, the harder it would be to turn back. San Felipe was the only town Neil and I had made it to all those years ago. One, because Bertha was on the fritz (as she almost always was), and two, because Neil had to get back to Utah for work. He only got a few days off for the trip. But I didn't have anywhere to be. I had quit my nine-to-five at a software company by then. I was actually starting to make a livable wage off of Instagram. I could have stayed there for a year, for all anyone cared. I remember thinking that to myself as I looked out the window while

Neil drove us back north toward the border. It had been the first time in my life that I felt inhibited by him instead of emboldened.

Ten minutes later, when the next stretch of beach appeared around the winding cliffside corners with San Felipe far in the rear-view mirror, I stopped the car. The dogs funneled out and tore off toward the seabirds that were standing one-legged in the last of the low tide. I sat there silently, my toes buried in white sand, tears streaming down my face. I was still sad . . . but I was so proud. I had officially made it farther alone than we had ever made it together.

I was familiar with *how* the security checkpoints in Baja worked; I just didn't realize how many of them there were along the length of the peninsula. These never put a real dent in my travel time, however, because it was July—nearly one hundred degrees every day, and nary a tourist in sight. Many of the security checkpoints were closed down entirely. I'd pull up to a faded red *Alto* sign, and I'd wait. Even if the checkpoint was very clearly abandoned, I still considered that, perhaps, some guy kicked back with his boots up somewhere would begrudgingly grab his AK-47 and come strolling out. A checkpoint between Guerrero Negro and Santa Rosalita was the first one that looked abandoned but was most certainly not.

At the sound of my squeaking brakes, three armed soldiers in full khaki-colored camouflage, complete with helmets and rifles, emerged from behind what appeared to either have once been, or might soon become, a bathroom. They were certainly intimidating looking. It reminded me of old photos of my grandfather when he fought in Desert

Storm. In Baja, the military patrols the streets as casually and as often as your average cop car rolls down Main Streets all over the United States. It's just to make their presence known, to keep a sense of perceived order. They stand in the back of Hummers and pickup trucks, painted in the same desert camouflage as the soldiers they carry. AK-47s half their size hung from their shoulders, but sometimes they had them resting casually on the sides of the truck bed, still technically aimed at everything they passed. In the often vast nothingness surrounding them, they somehow seemed tougher than your average soldiers. Or, perhaps, I'd just never been around so many soldiers.

I rolled my window down, smiling wide. "Holaaa!" I sung, as I always did. It was the only Spanish word I ever said with full confidence that I was actually saying it correctly. Two of the officers stood at my driver's side window, the third at the passenger, which was occupied by Birdie and Banjo scrambling over each other to inspect the man outside the window with the gun. I shushed them in time to hear the obligatory questions they always ask first. "De dónde vienes?" (Where are you coming from?) and "Adónde vas?" (Where are you going?). I only knew for certain that *dondé* meant "where," the rest I just assumed. Once I'd answered, I sat—still smiling—looking from face to face. They stared back, seemingly amused.

Traveling alone as a woman isn't exactly *revolutionary*, but it is still seen as unusual in many foreign countries. Sometimes I felt just as amused as they were. There hadn't been a single hour that had gone by in the past few days where I didn't laugh out loud at the fact that I had just thrown some clothes and a paddleboard into my Jeep, and—without any real plan, timeline, or a lick of understanding of the Spanish language—

took off into another country with a *let's just see what happens* attitude. Regardless, each time I pulled up to an occupied checkpoint, it was very apparent that the soldiers were not used to seeing a tall blonde driving alone through the desert with a trunk full of dogs.

I was never *afraid* of the soldiers or the searches they'd perform on passing vehicles. Though I had heard about a bit of a stickup from some friends not too long ago. They were at a military checkpoint when a soldier found the tail end of a forgotten joint on the floorboard of their van. The soldiers swarmed them, all hands on deck, demanding they get out of the vehicle. They screamed that the Mexican police were coming, that they were going to be taken to prison. My friends were terror-stricken. But moments later, one of the soldiers pulled them aside and said they would let it slide for two hundred US dollars. They handed him the cash and they were let on their way with the whole crew of soldiers waving them off as if nothing had ever happened. I'd yet to have any particularly negative experience, myself, so I wasn't frightened by the process.

One soldier opened my driver's side door, motioning for me to get out. This, too, was still normal. Checkpoint guards ask people to get out of their vehicles all the time, and at random, no less. Sometimes they'd lean in and take a quick scan of your car's contents, other times they'd practically tear it apart. More often than not, they'd just wave you forward. But after I'd stepped out, they asked me to get the dogs out too. All of them. "Why so many dog?" one asked me, in broken English, as I fumbled for the leashes that were buried in the car somewhere, untouched since I'd crossed the border. "Cómo se dice . . . divorce?" I asked, laughing at my own joke. He didn't laugh because he either didn't understand or didn't think it was funny. Which one, I'll never know.

The soldiers looked through my car thoroughly enough to have dog hair stuck to their uniforms by the time they were finished. I loaded the dogs back up, unclipping their leashes one by one. *Okay, load up. Load up. Load up. Load up.* I stood with my arm outstretched, directing each one into the car like an usher in a theater. Several of the soldiers chuckled, resting their forearms on the guns hanging across their torsos. I stepped around to the driver's side, still smiling far more than the situation called for. "Eh! Eh!" one soldier yelled, holding up a finger. What he said next, I didn't know. To this day, I still don't know. He said something—a full sentence—in Spanish. I stared back, my mouth open as if about to reply. "Umm . . ." I looked from his face to another's. "What? No comprendé. Lo siento!" (*Lo siento* means I'm sorry, and that was probably my second most uttered word besides *Hola. Sorry* gets you a long way in a lot of places.) He repeated the question again, slowly, but still entirely in Spanish. "I uhh . . . I'm sorry err lo siento I don't . . ." I trailed off. He repeated the sentence once more, but mimed something with his hands that looked like opening a book.

"Passport?!" I asked, turning to dig into my glovebox. I handed over my passport. He took it and held it up to show another soldier, saying something I—again—didn't understand. But then he shook his head. One by one I handed over every single piece of paper in that glovebox. Car insurance. Registration. Visa. The dogs' veterinary records I'd printed off to prove they weren't rabid. Each time he shrugged. Every time I turned around, his face seemed to grow more hopeless. It is crucial to note that there was absolutely no cell phone service, and certainly no Wi-Fi. Google Translate wasn't an option. There . . . was no option. We were quite literally at an impasse. We both looked from face to face, horizon to horizon, shrugging at each other. Finally, I couldn't take it anymore. I burst out laughing, tossing my hands up as if to say, *Okay, I give up.* The soldiers started laughing too. The one holding all my papers shrugged back at me and handed everything over.

After closing the glovebox, I moved my hand slowly toward the key. It seemed illegal to just . . . drive away. I was still half-expecting handcuffs to come out if I started the car for failing to answer whatever the hell I was being asked. But they just looked on, still seemingly entertained. "Okay, well . . . Adiós!"

Being a woman on your own is a fine line to walk . . . a juggling act of how to use the things that can be both helpful *and* dangerous. I could play clueless when I needed to, toss my hands up like the old dumb blond trope if it would help me get out of a sticky situation. But sometimes, I really *was* clueless. This wasn't Cancún. This wasn't some resort designed to cater to white people on vacation. There were towns down there where most people spoke no English at all because they simply had no need to. And I had just waltzed in and expected to float by on smiles and a handful of poorly pronounced words. And thus far, I had.

Playing dumb didn't felt dangerous yet. And if it did, I'd just have to pretend that I wasn't. I'd have to pretend that I wasn't afraid. I'd have to switch on my other starring role: the gruff, callous woman. The woman who can handle her own. The woman who didn't need anybody. I much preferred that role anyway.

chapter sixteen

The Beach

One afternoon, I started piling up my usual supplies for the day. The paddleboard. The cooler. The umbrella I'd bought on the side of the road after having the seller type the physical numbers into my calculator app because I didn't know how much "cuatrocientos" was, no matter how many times he said it. I grabbed a drybag for my phone and my book. Treats for the dogs. Sunscreen. Something to drink.

I'd been down there for over three weeks by then, so this routine had become mindless. It was what we did most every day. Wake up, make coffee, and zoom in and out on satellite maps and overlanding apps for an hour or so, looking for beaches. Beaches that belonged only to us for a day. Beaches that were only accessible from the water. I would paddle us up to a mile, sometimes more, to little strips of white sand on a rock just big enough to be called an island. For seemingly no reason at all, the sharp, rocky slopes abruptly turned to powdered sugar sand. The contrast of the barren, red desert was stark against the tropical, turquoise water so teeming with life that Jacques Cousteau called the Sea of Cortez "the aquarium of the world."

Beneath the buzz of dry heat, and prickly plant life, lay a world that could not be more different. Sixty-one thousand square miles of cerulean sea with nine hundred different species of fish and at least forty-three species of marine mammals. I didn't even know that stingrays could fly until I sat on a paddleboard out there.

The previous two days, we'd gone to the same beach. It was my favorite so far, but I figured I should explore a bit more if I was going to lean in to this new person I was becoming. I spotted a beach that was tucked on the south side of a peninsula that appeared to have some sort of radio tower on top of it. There looked to be the faintest two-track road through the dirt, but it ended at the tower and went nowhere near the beach. *Just folks who check the tower from time to time, probably,* I said to the dogs as I zoomed in as close as the screen would let me.

They sat—almost in a perfect row—across the white tiles in front of the door. I had already packed the bags, so they knew *exactly* what we were about to do, and they were very confused as to why we had not yet started doing it. Having dogs and having kids are different in many ways, but if dogs spoke English, I guarantee they'd ask *Are we there yet?* Far more than any human child ever has. There was a clear pull-off on the side of the closest road that seemed like a good spot to leave the car. I'd just have to paddle us through the mangroves, but based on the tide, that could either be a breeze or a total nightmare. I googled the chart, and was thrilled to find that high tide had been only an hour or so ago. *Woohoo! Let's go, kids!*

When we arrived, I kept the dogs in the Jeep with the AC running. Not only for the heat, but for the fact that the pull-off was just a few feet off the road and the occasional car that would pass seemed to always be doing so at reckless speeds. I stood beside the steaming pavement, blowing up the paddleboard with my manual pump, sweat pouring from my face. A honking horn startled me. I looked up just in time to see an old red pickup truck with three men across the bench seat of the cab, and another three sitting atop a pile of mattresses that appeared to be strapped to a pile of old kitchen appliances that was strapped to the rusted bed of the truck. They threw a wave. One blew a kiss.

Once I'd finished inflating the board, I went about the task of trying to carry everything at once. Eventually, I'd strap it all to the board—which looked equally as absurd, I might add—but if I strapped it all to the board right there, it would be too heavy for me to carry down to the water. I always had to make two trips. The dogs howled when I set off on the first trip. I had backpacks and bags hanging off of both arms, an umbrella and a paddle tucked under each. It must have looked as though I was headed off on this great adventure without them. *I'll be riiiight back. I'm coming riiiight back*, I shouted over my shoulder. I doubt they could hear me over themselves.

Only on my second trip down to the water did I realize it

should have been three. I had the paddleboard under one arm, and four leashes dragging the other. I knew they'd hop right on, but we were far too close to the road to risk any funny business. They were a hell storm on leash. So much so that every time they were on one, I became acutely aware that four dogs is *a lot* of dogs. But man, did I love 'em. *Okay, load up!* I said, watching them enthusiastically leap up onto the board, soaking every single item I had just arranged. Bucket claimed the bow of the board, her front paws dangling ever so slightly into the passing water. Birdie stood with her head between my thighs, turning toward every bird that flew up from the mangroves. Dagwood curled up right behind my ankles, facing the water behind us. That boy always had my six. Banjo looked at each of them, seemingly deciding whose behavior to mimic. He was still relatively new to this, after all.

With the exception of an alarming amount of plastic garbage tucked between the occasional clump of seaweed, the beach was a dream. If you squinted past the bags and bottles, it looked like something from a Sandals honeymoon commercial. We walked from one end to the other and then back again. And then back again. I'd been on my own for a good while, by then, and had grown better at filling the time. Some folks might have looked at how I spent my days and found it quite boring. On the surface it appeared that I was, for the most part, doing a whole lotta nothing. But I think some folks just have a different definition of "nothing" than I do.

I could spend a whole day just wandering around looking at stuff. I never needed a trail, a high peak, a conquest, a distance, a goal. I'd just end up where I ended up when I ended up there. Doing nothing requires you to be surprisingly present. And if you want to learn to be present, you should surround yourself with dogs. *How could you possibly say there's nothing to do when there's nothing NOT to do!?* I could imagine Dagwood saying. *There's a perfectly good dead puffer fish over there that we could be looking at as we speak!* Perhaps human children bring this out in people too, but unlike humans, dogs never outgrow that kind of simple, unbridled joy. They never get bored with it. A head out the car window will always be just as good as it was the first time.

By afternoon, the sun was low enough to cast a little bit of shade next to the boulder I was lying beside. Bucket happily dug herself a sandy den and curled up against it. Flat on my back, I held a book up with one hand, using the other to block the sun. I was reading *Women Who Run with the Wolves* again, but I must have started to doze off because the sudden uproar of barking seemed more startling than it usually did.

I shot up, my towel sticking to the sweat on my back. The dogs were sprinting so fast, I could scarcely see anything besides four clouds of kicked-up sand. It took a moment or two, but eventually my eyes adjusted. At the far end of the white sand beach stood a completely naked man. I, myself, was topless (as I always was) so my first priority was to hurriedly cover up. He was still far away, but close enough to see that I had done so. "S'okay!" he shouted in a thick accent, using his own chest to mime the action of taking my top back off. The dogs had stopped just a few dozen yards away from him, barking wildly. Despite immediately feeling uneasy, I called out, "Lo siento!! Friendly! Friendly!" At the moment, they certainly didn't *look* friendly. But he didn't seem to notice them at all. His eyes were locked in on me.

I called the dogs' names out one by one and eventually, all but Birdie headed back toward me, stopping every now and again to peer over their shoulders cautiously. But not Birdie. Birdie stood squarely in front of him. She never took her eyes off of him. She mirrored his every step as he waded into the water. He had a black mesh bag over his shoulder, presumably for clamming. *He's just clamming*, I said to Dagwood as I patted his head. He had returned to my side, pressed up close against my leg, despite the heat that radiated from both of us. I kept my face dropped low in my book, shifting my eyes upward every few seconds from behind the mirrored lenses of my sunglasses.

Each and every time, he was staring directly at me. Each and every time, he was getting closer. He waded, waist deep, in the turquoise water, his penis occasionally bobbing on the surface. I felt sick to my stomach. I stared at the page of my book, not reading a single word. Eventually, he got close enough for the other three dogs to rejoin Birdie. They erupted in a barking fit again, as though they'd just seen him for the first time.

He stood out in the water ten feet or more. They barked and lunged from the place where the sand became the sea. Still, he waded over until he was almost directly in front of me, but still in deep enough to where the dogs couldn't reach him. It felt akin to being hunted, the way an animal cases its prey. I knew he'd have to have a death wish to come much closer. I knew all four of them would become practically rabid at the slightest sound of my scream. But still he stood there, looking down at the water, mimicking someone doing something normal for long enough that Dagwood lay back down again. Bucket retreated to her shady nook beneath the rock, digging down into the cool sand and settling in. Banjo resumed chewing on the rotting corpse of a triggerfish the low tide had gifted him with. His attention span was, after all, still only that of a six-month-old puppy.

I lay, staring into the same book page for ten minutes straight. It felt like I was holding my breath the entire time. I had told someone where I was. My mom had my location tracked on her phone, but my phone had been in airplane mode since I left the Airbnb hours—and miles—ago. *She's going to kill me if I don't come back*, I thought to myself, which is an absurd thought given that it would be hard to kill your daughter if she was already dead.

After some time had gone by, the man started calling out to me, motioning for me to come toward him. Unlike the others, Birdie had still not stepped away from him. She sat right on the sand, staring him down, not moving an inch. He called out to me again. With a low growl, Birdie stepped into the water up to her chest. The man took a big step back, but was still pointing at the gallon jug of drinking water I had beside me. "Agua? Por favor?" He wanted water. I had water. I had half a gallon left. He could see it plain as day. It would be cruel to not give him water if he was just thirsty, but everything in my body told me he was not just thirsty and that bottle was not what he was really trying to get to.

It was in this moment that I defaulted to one of the more

dangerous positions women put themselves in. I was scared, but I didn't want to be rude. I didn't want to be dramatic. I didn't want to be killed, as women so often are, for the mere act of rejecting some kind of advance. All I could muster was "Lo siento," as I stood to start packing up my things. He continued yelling out to me in Spanish, but I couldn't hear him over the dogs barking and the sound of my own breathing. I didn't want to look frantic, because that also seemed rude. Only when I dropped half the contents of my bag onto the sand did I realize that he was laughing at me. A laugh I'll never forget as long as I live. A laugh that made every hair on my body stand up.

Birdie seemed to grow more agitated by the second. Her lips were curled so high, it looked like she had more gum than she did teeth. Her fur stood upright, tail cocked, every muscle rippling. She looked like a different dog. She looked terrifying. And that terrified me even more. She lunged at him twice. Once when he took another step toward me, and again when he swung his arm as if to swat her away. I had dragged the paddleboard to the water and Bucket and Dagwood had already jumped on. They were standing fully postured in his direction. Bucket had started barking now too, which startled Banjo as he clambered his way up over the backpacks I'd tossed on. I had begun to cry, but I tried to hide that too.

I shoved the board off the shore as hard as I could with my paddle and yelled out to Birdie. She turned on a dime. Her eyes only left him for a split second as she leapt aboard. Her body, still half-soaked and bristling, spun right back toward him. Her head was crouched low, in line with her whole spine. Her front leg looked poised to pounce.

I paddled as fast as I could. Birdie and Banjo were on the board behind me, Bucket and Dagwood in front. It was only a few strokes later that the man started whistling. I turned my head to see him clapping his hands, calling out as if baby-talking to the dogs. Banjo stood on the end of the paddleboard that was closest to the shore, tail wagging. His front paws looked as though they might leap at any second. I reared back and grabbed ahold of his tail so fast, he yelped. I plopped him between my legs and paddled furiously, sitting cross-legged on the board as bags dangled and floated haphazardly all around us. I didn't have time to tie anything down. *I'm sorry, Banj, I'm sorry honey. It's okay, it's okay*, I cried.

I didn't paddle back to the car. I paddled straight out. Straight out into the deep water until the shoreline behind us got small. When I finally stopped, I cupped my hands over my face and cried. The dogs rushed to comfort me so feverishly, we nearly capsized. Birdie sat peering over my shoulder, licking every inch of skin she could reach. In no time at all, she had returned to who I'd always known her to be. An awkward, lanky, submissive puddle of a dog whose ears looked like Dobby the house elf from the Harry Potter movies. She glanced up at me, her face still downcast. She looked confused, scared even. It looked as though she wasn't sure if she had done something wrong. The fear seemed to overtake her the same way it had overtaken me. We reverted to instinct. I wrapped my arms around her, pulling her into my chest. Her fur was still damp and warm from the sun. I could taste the salt when I kissed her forehead.

. . .

That night, I lay in the hammock on the roof of my Airbnb . . . and I blamed myself. Blaming myself was all I knew how to do anymore. Who did I think I was, just gallivanting off to a place where I couldn't speak the language? If I had been able to communicate, maybe I could have told him he was making me uncomfortable. Maybe I could have said, "You better leave before my dog rips your fucking throat out." I glanced down at Birdie, asleep on the warm tiles beneath me in the last of the day's sun.

If *I* knew how to speak Spanish, then that wouldn't have happened. If *I* hadn't been so angry after my dad left, maybe he would have tried harder to have a relationship with me. If *I* had known how much Neil was drinking, I could have intervened. If *I* hadn't been so preoccupied with posting on Instagram, I might have seen what was happening to my marriage. If *I* had just told the truth about Dagwood's accident in the first place, maybe there would be no subreddit, no harassment, no stalking . . .

Blaming myself had become a form of survival. If everything was *my* fault, that meant I had some sort of control over it . . . that meant I could make sense of it, fix it, never let it happen again. But this form of "survival" I was so hell-bent on had come quite close to potentially killing me that day. Because the reality is, that naked man on the beach didn't need to speak English to see that I was absolutely terrified. The reality is, I was *sixteen years old* when my father left. The reality is, I'm not a mind reader. Neil was a grown man who made all of his own choices. The reality is, Instagram wasn't just some hobby

I was distracting myself with . . . it had become my career. And if I had never posted about the accident, there would never have been any donations. If I had never posted about the accident, Dagwood would have died. The reality is, it was an accident, and *I* was the one who saved my dog's life. Anyone who wouldn't have done the same has never truly loved a dog. And anyone who terrorizes a stranger for years on end about that is a monster. Anyone who joins a "like-minded community" about that has lost their humanity entirely.

Nothing—none of this—had been "all my fault" as I'd cried to my therapist so many, many times. Control is a comforting idea to cling to until you realize it never existed in the first place.

On the staircase of my childhood home, there was a photo of my dad and two of his brothers: wide smiles, aviator sunglasses, arms draped over each other's tanned shoulders. They had kissed their wives and young kids goodbye and jetted off on the ultimate adventure together, driving down into Mexico to travel the Baja peninsula. They were probably about the age that I was as I lay in the hammock that night. As I sat looking out at the Sea of Cortez, with a patchwork of salt-covered hounds at my feet, I wondered what that little girl in the stairwell would think of us now. I wonder if she could have ever imagined all of this—the good, the bad, the beautiful, the disastrous—all of it. But I know that little girl well. I'm sure all she'd care about was that I'd kept so many of my promises. Most importantly, the one about surrounding myself with dogs. Nothing in the world felt safer than that.

chapter seventeen

The Will

Just a few months before I drove to Baja, I had an appointment in Moab. Since I had acquired something of actual monetary value, my mother insisted I meet with an estate planner. She was so adamant about it, in fact, that she called and scheduled it on my behalf. I conceded, thinking that I could very well be dead soon anyway. She called daily in the week leading up to said appointment with demands for various passwords so she could prepare me. She logged in to my bank accounts, my 401(k), my car insurance, my health insurance . . . anything that Neil still had access to or, worse, was still listed as the beneficiary for. She changed passwords and usernames and security questions, excising the final slivers of him from my life with a series of keyboard clicks. I wouldn't be surprised if she went as far as to change my Netflix password. My mother is unbelievably efficient in times of crisis. By the time the meeting rolled around, she had emailed me everything I would need.

Regardless, my paperwork was simple. I decided that the land would go to my mother. Any money I had would go to my brother and his kids. And Bertha would go to my mom so I could die laughing at the thought of her driving that massive orange thing around the pristine streets of Connecticut. The estate planner sat across the desk from me, perplexed, fingers hovered over her keyboard, before saying, "So Bertha is . . . a car, I take it?" I often forgot that not everyone knew Bertha by name, that not everyone knew her as this one-named idol like Cher or Madonna.

She seemed quite annoyed by my demeanor, which was positively blasé. This was a serious conversation, but nothing ever felt serious to me anymore. This was a meeting about dying. But once I was dead, I'd just be . . . dead. None of this would even matter. That was the whole point of being dead. That's what was so appealing about it.

"These details will be important if, God forbid, something ever happened to you," she said, almost scoldingly. She sounded like my mother. And just like my mother, I doubt she had any idea that something *was* going to happen to me. I doubt she knew I had bought a handgun at a sporting goods store the last time I'd been in Salt Lake City. She thought we were planning for the unthinkable. I was planning for the inevitable.

On at least four different occasions over the previous weeks, I had sat holding it on my lap, trying to work up the courage. On one of those occasions, the barrel had made it all the way up to my temple before I chickened out. I wasn't even certain I had loaded the bullets right, anyway. I had stood at the counter of that sporting goods store knowing not one thing about guns. The man behind it never asked why I wanted one or what I planned to use it for. I wonder what I would have said if he had. Instead, I just pointed to some long-barrel six-shooter in the glass case that looked like something John Wayne would have had. *I'm gonna go out like a cowboy*, I said to the dogs, when I got back in the car.

Death was all around us out there in the desert. The bleached-white ribcage of an open-range bull. The jawbone of a pronghorn. Tattered, cracking wings outstretched on either side of what was once a turkey vulture. Death appears as an inseparable part of the desert landscape, a pattern in the very fabric of the environment. Any old clip art search for "desert" is chock-full of that cliché cow skull leaned up against a saguaro cactus. In the desert, death is decorative. After all, it seems easier to die in a place like that than it is to live. As I drove back toward the mesa that afternoon, it was comforting to know that I'd still fit in out there, even after I was gone.

I was staring absentmindedly out the window when the estate planner asked me who would take care of them. "What?" I said, suddenly, whipping my head back toward her. She repeated the question. "If you pass away before your dogs do, who would you like their care designated to?" I was taken aback, almost *offended* by what she had said. I fell completely silent. After a full thirty seconds of staring at the carpet between my feet, I stuttered, "Well . . . there are *four* of them . . ."

"We can always designate different caretakers for each if—"

"They're not being separated," I snapped, cutting her off. I felt nauseous. "Wait, wait . . ." I stuttered, "I'm not . . . I don't . . ." I didn't even know what I was attempting to say. It just suddenly felt so . . . real. Like a record scratch, like someone flicking on fluorescent lights in the dark room you've been feeling your way through. I reached out with both hands, physically holding on to the edge of the desk. My mind raced.

Who would they live with? Where would they live? They certainly couldn't live in the city. But who would agree to move out to the desert and live in a trailer just to upkeep the lifestyle of four unruly dogs?

"I . . . don't know," I choked out through gritted teeth. I was doing my best to hold back tears, but it wasn't too successful. They welled, hot and stinging, in the corners of my eyes. The estate planner seemed to soften. "These are tough questions, Ms. Madia, you don't have to know all these answers now, and you can always *change* these answers down the road as you see fit."

I nodded slowly, staring at the carpet again, imagining what the dogs would think if they just . . . never saw me again. If I just up and disappeared one day. I wondered if Dagwood would run after every passing Jeep too, hoping beyond hope that it might be me coming back for him. I hope they wouldn't think it was their fault. I hope they wouldn't think it was something they did wrong.

Back in my car, I fumbled for my keys, still fighting back tears. I had a few more errands I had planned to run while I was in town, but I hooked a hard left out of the parking lot instead. I drove as fast as I could back up to the mesa, staring straight over the steering wheel, steeped in thought. My happiness was dependent on the dogs' happiness but I seemed to have forgotten that they were dependent on me for theirs.

Perhaps it sounds strange, but I never really saw them as "needing" me. I thought of them as a wholly separate entity . . . a sort of mythical thing. The stuff of legends. "Well at least I know they'd survive, they'd clearly be able to find food," I'd say each and every time they'd kill some rodent. "They're tough, they're wild, they belong out here!" Sure, the four of them could eat or protect each other or stay warm, but their *happiness*? That *was* my responsibility. They couldn't live this life without me. There would be no days down by the river, no weeks of doing all that glorious nothing, no bike rides, no strolling the grounds, no dog-hair-filled Jeep that charioted them around from one beautiful place to another. They needed me just as much as I needed them.

Thirty minutes later, I was tearing up my driveway, dust clouds dancing off of each tire. The dogs erupted in frenzied howling. I could hear Birdie waiting by the door, her tail whack-whack-whacking against the side of the stove. Banjo's face burst between the curtains, standing on the table he's not supposed to stand on. I flung the door open and they burst through the screen flap, nearly toppling me to the ground. Bucket ran in small zoomy circles, her nails skidding across the wooden deck. Banjo wriggled his rear end, squealing with high-pitched puppy joy. Birdie army-crawled beneath everyone else to get to me as quickly and as sneakily as she could. Dagwood hopped up on his back legs, tossing his little lion paws up over each of my shoulders: a feat not so easy with his plated leg and all that scar tissue. A feat reserved for special occasions . . . like me getting out of the shower, or coming home after being gone for *one whole hour*, or just the times when he suddenly remembered that I was there with him, suddenly remembered how happy he was for that.

I lay there on the wooden deck coated in dirt and dog hair, their wet jowls resting on my arms, velvet soft ears on my chest. I closed my eyes, breathing in the warmth of them. And that was all it took. That settled it. I decided right then and there that I just . . . couldn't die.

At least not before them.

ACKNOWLEDGMENTS

To William, for the penny, the clover, and the ring. And for bringing me back to the present on days when I've struggled with the past. And to my mother, for loving me through things only a mother could.

I would not be here to write this book without my best friend, Mary Scinto. Thank you for everything that you are. Thank you to all of my beloved friends whose paths I've been lucky enough to have cross with mine. You are my family.

My books are only made possible because of my wonderful agent Abby Saul and her Monday morning check-ins. Thank you to my editor, Gabriella Page-Fort, and my entire team at Harper-One. And a special thank-you to Sydney Rogers as well for her guidance.

To Susan, for never tiring of reminding me to forgive myself.

ACKNOWLEDGMENTS

To the entire staff of Underdog Rescue Moab: thank you for what you do.

To the wonderful people who have followed along with my stories on Instagram for so many years now: your kindness means more to me than you may ever know.

And to my beloved little town of Moab . . . stay weird.

ABOUT THE AUTHOR

BRIANNA MADIA has lived a life of relentless intention, traveling the deserts of the American West in an old Ford van. She made a name for herself on social media with her inspiring captions-cum-essays about bravery, identity, nature, and subverting expectations. She lives in Utah with her four dogs. Her first book, *Nowhere for Very Long*, was a *New York Times* bestseller. *Never Leave the Dogs Behind* is her second book.